THE ART OF SOCIAL INTELLIGENCE

OBSERVE THE HABITS OF HIGHLY EFFECTIVE PEOPLE AND IMPROVE YOUR MINDSET

JOHN WARD

John Ward

"The way to do is to be."

Lao Tzu

CONTENTS

Fostering professional and personal relationships can be quite a challenge to some. However, there are people who seem to just breeze right through the process. The task of socializing and connecting seem so effortless to them. Have you ever wondered what makes these people different?

The answer to that is social intelligence. The reason why it seems so natural for these people to start great conversations and create a good social network is that they have high social literacy. Social intelligence gives individuals the ability to approach social situations better by equipping them with the ability to assess all the elements in these interactions.

These individuals are able to sense the emotional state of their peers. They are able to respond to social dynamics appropriately. They have a good sense of self-awareness and are self-assured even in the most hectic situations. They are also able to express their ideas more effectively and their peers respond more positively to them.

Acquiring social literacy gives individuals an advantage both in their professional and personal lives. With it, the difficulty in understanding your boss, your partner, your friends, and your family becomes much less. You will be able to have a better perspective of yourself, your relationships, and your engagements with others by simply using the devices you will learn as you develop your social intelligence. Having the ability to effectively address your social relations will eventually give you a happier, more rewarding, and more fulfilling life.

The good news is that social intelligence can be developed. It is not set and it can be worked on as long as you have the right mindset for it. Being socially literate is not something you are simply born with. You can develop the right set of skills to harness it and that is what this book aims to provide you with.

However, developing social intelligence is not a replacement for a person's sense of identity. Before we delve into the intricacies of interacting with others, we will first go through the process of honest self-discovery and forming your own personal brand.

This is the prerequisite to building relationships with others. You must first have a sense of self that is authentic and true. This will enable you to keep your interactions genuine and sincere. It will also make you aware of the bad habits and damaging mistakes you make in the way you socialize with others.

Authenticity plays a big role in being able to develop your self-awareness and self-esteem. Both of which are important aspects of honing your social intelligence. The journey to getting to know yourself will require you to be more honest in the way you view yourself and the things that you do.

It is impossible to understand yourself if you are only basing your self-worth and identity on the approval of others. It will be very important for you to commit to honest self-reflection as you follow the book. It is the only way for you to understand how all the teachings can be applied in your life. The most important thing is that you use these lessons to live your true sense of self.

Social literacy cannot be instantly acquired. You do not just define it and you instantly have the tools and skills you need. It takes a lot of practice and commitment. That commitment can only come if you participate in a way that is authentic to you.

This book will not focus solely on the philosophical path toward social intelligence. Instead, it will include actual instructions and practical steps you can take. We will delve into the actions you have to make to really develop your skills and widen your perspective on things.

One of the things you will learn in this book is the difference between effective communication and communication that is only meant to please your peers. If you approach every single conversation with the mindset that you are going to get the other person's approval, you will likely end up disappointing yourself.

Although you can get people to like you with it, there is a more important aspect you can learn as you polish up on your social intelligence and that is setting appropriate goals within your interactions. This can be a variety of things like planning a project, understanding a concept you are working on, or maybe even just having a great time enjoying someone else's company. Having a good understanding of your social goals can make you more effective and less anxious when it comes to social interactions.

The best tool you can have in any social setting is to be able to communicate effectively. Effective communication includes verbal and nonverbal language. Each will be discussed in the book thoroughly. Improving your communication skills will be an important part of social literacy.

One way you can look at social literacy is in the form of intuition. After you practice all the steps and you commit to them, you eventually develop an instinct for it. Soon enough, you will look at all social interactions in a better light and respond to them more intuitively because you have acquired a set of habits that are proven to be effective. Eventually, you will also see a difference in the way people respond to your communication.

The greatest difficulty in social interactions is that people are raised differently and you have to have a different approach from person to person. To do that, you must have a way to separate yourself from the differences you have with other people.

That can be daunting, of course. If you look at it as a whole bunch of people that you have to study and figure out before you even approach them, you will be overwhelmed. That is why we will keep going back to your own identity. The best way for you to understand others is knowing that you yourself have your own values, beliefs, culture, and needs. And once you shift your attention to other people, you will find out how similar and different people can be from each other.

Because of our differences in culture and beliefs, conflicts become inevitable. That is why conflict resolution is one of the important things that will be tackled in this book. It is easy to damage relationships when conflict resolutions do not work out. But resolving conflicts is not an impossible task and as long as it is approached with respect and effective communication is applied, it can be a rewarding process that can further strengthen relationships. That is where social literacy does its work best.

Emotional intelligence also plays a crucial part in gaining social literacy. Although they have their similarities, emotional intelligence confronts ideas, and concepts surrounding the emotions of a person and social intelligence is more about understanding individuals and how they interact with others.

The intricacies of emotional intelligence and how to improve on it will be discussed because it is essential for a person to see and understand how emotions can affect the way people interact in social settings and how feelings can be better managed so that individuals can navigate through socializing without being taken over by strong emotions.

Emotional intelligence can also further a person's viewpoint on the relationships he or she engages in. By being more in touch with his own emotions and those of others, a person gets to appreciate other people more for who they really are outside of the situations and processes they are in.

Our lives go through a lot of ups and downs and these struggles can affect our ability to be true to ourselves and to be available for new learnings and self-enrichment. Lessons on how we can be able to regain control of our lives and look forward to a more fulfilling future will also be a part of this learning journey towards social intelligence.

When we are able to manage our lives better and let go of the fears and self-doubt that mistakes from the past come with, we are enabled to further our learnings and develop a stronger sense of independence.

Throughout my career as a psychology professor and as a motivational speaker, I have been approached numerous times by people who are having trouble with self-defeating habits when it comes to understanding themselves, understanding other people, and being able to create meaningful connections.

When I was younger, I myself have struggled with my communication skills. As I grew up and learned more about people, what motivates them, and what holds them back from the things they aspire to be, I found how improving one's social intelligence can help people get ahead in life, form worthwhile relationships, and allow themselves to be free from negativity and self-doubt.

Social intelligence can be challenging to master but if you approach it proactively, you can reap the benefits more quickly. With this book, you will be able to get rid of your fears and anxieties when it comes to socializing and working with other people. This book aims to help you understand yourself and others more so that you can identify what skills and devices you can tap into for a more fulfilling and effective social life.

UNDERSTAND YOURSELF

*I*magine yourself in a hallway and then a classmate from 10 years ago suddenly pops up out of nowhere. After you realize who this person was, you start to associate his current self to your previous encounters with him. He appears to be your classmate who stuttered when he spoke. You prep yourself with the same methods you chose when you interacted with him in the past.

Once you started a conversation with him, you expected him to have the same speech problems he had when you were younger. You tell yourself to be kind and to try your best not to look bothered once he starts to stutter.

As he opens his mouth, he speaks to you in perfect speech without stumbling. You find out from him that he was able to overcome his stutter and is no longer struggling with his speech.

Your brain then goes into refocus as you discover that what you know about this other person in the past is no longer true in the present.

All the prepping you did as you anticipated your exchange with him was based on a preset that was formed from the past and was revisited by your brain. The initial concepts you had were processed within your own mind and held no proof of what was to come but you still decided to curate your actions based on them.

Three aspects of a person's being can affect how he manages relationships and interactions with his peers. These are social, mental, and physical aspects.

Let's break down the encounter with the class-mate. The social aspect was the acknowledgment that your classmate is a person who is separate from you and that he is capable of interacting with you. He is not an inanimate object that won't be bothered if you just walk past them.

Once you recognize this person, several thoughts ran through your head and everything about that person comes from a collection of memories of previously having his presence around. You were reminded of his voice, his gestures, and his looks.

These are all social elements and you attach these references to that person's being.

Then, there's the mental aspect. When you started making conclusions and decisions about this person, it was your mind that came up with those things. Your brain has processed the information that was gathered from the past and it led you to decide on the actions you will be taking in the current situation.

You could not have possibly telepathically communicated with your former classmate –if you did, you would have found out that he no longer stutters when he speaks. All the ideas that influenced your actions were all in your mind.

The third is the physical aspect. The common reflex action when you see a person you know is raising your eyebrows. The next thing may be waving at them or smiling at them. These are physical responses your body makes when placed in such situations.

These three aspects work together and their effects may not always seem obvious to you but they matter. Before you even get to the other person, your mind and body have already reacted. How a person acts in social interactions comes from internal thoughts and preexisting notions.

To be able to understand your social environment, it is most important to understand yourself first. This process is called introspection. Introspection works by looking within you and assessing your own thoughts and emotions. The process allows you to gain knowledge about yourself and this knowledge can only come from self-reflection and self-analysis. Introspection can help make the connections between experiences and how people respond to your behavior.

To do this, there are some questions you can ask yourself.

NUMBER 1: HOW DO YOU REACT WHEN A STRANGER GREETS YOU?

Say, a random person comes up to you at the grocery and says, "Hi". Do you smile? Do you greet them back?

Seeing how you respond to these kinds of situations can help you assess the first impression you give to other people. This stranger will receive the first information he can get about you. What will be the first adjective he gives you? Are you a snub? Are you polite? Are you awkward?

NUMBER 2: HOW DO YOU RESPOND TO SOCIAL STIMULI?

The stranger in the grocery asks you if you are vegan. What thoughts run through your head as this person talks to you? Are you setting expectations? Do you feel anxious? Are there physical manifestations of your reactions like stuttering or maybe a change in the tone and pitch of your voice? What reflexes do you start to show?

During the encounters you've had in the past, do you find that certain people, topics, or environments make you respond a certain way? Say your pet peeve would be high pitched voices, does your aversion to that affect the way you socialize with people?

All of these questions in number two are triggered by outside influence or stimuli. These can only be determined by the reactions you've shown towards previous social experiences.

NUMBER 3: IS YOUR SOCIAL BEHAVIOR REPULSIVE?

Now, this is when you start to look outside of yourself more. After participating in social interactions, how have people reacted to you? Were there instances when you negatively affected a person because of the way you handled your interactions with them?

There are certain cues you get when another person starts getting uncomfortable with you. One would be a negative change in their behavior or speech. Another one is when you do not get a second chance with this person anymore. He starts avoiding you and you do not ever continue on any form of relationship with him.

There are a lot more ways to tell if someone has responded negatively to socially interacting with you. See if you can figure out what actions came from you that led to this. Maybe you were too excited about something and you started sounding preachy when you spoke? Maybe you were just too happy and you didn't realize you were already talking over another person?

Try to look at the things you do that make you repulsive to other people. You may have been hurtful or obnoxious in the past and you just weren't aware of it.

NUMBER 4: DO YOU HAVE ANY BAD EXPERIENCES IN THE PAST WHEN IT COMES TO SOCIALIZING?

If you do, what happened during these encounters? Where in those particular instances did you start feeling it would turn bad? Are there words or actions that you would want to take back?

For example, it was a terrible argument with a friend. You were talking about who the stronger superhero is. It's Batman versus Superman. You were on Batman's side and your friend just couldn't agree with you. He suddenly starts yelling at you and then he walks out on you.

After having a second look at this situation, you remember that you were the first one who started raising your voice. Apparently, you were stressed out about other things that day and it made you a little too passionate about Batman in this situation.

Are you sorry for the way you handled this? Would you have done it differently?

How about if it was the other way around and you were in the shoes of your friend instead? You now realize that you were shocked that your friend had raised his voice so you started shouting in retaliation.

When you look back on this, would you have done the same thing? Do you still feel like your reaction was the right response?

NUMBER 5: WAS THERE EVER A TIME WHEN YOU FELT HAPPY AND CONFIDENT WITH THE OUTCOME OF A SOCIAL SITUATION?

Do you have favorite memories of conversations or moments spent with another person? Go back to those times. What made you happy during these encounters? Was it the other person's or your participation that made you enjoy this particular instance?

If it was your own actions that made you fulfilled, what actions or words do you think made the difference? Are you still applying those things today and are they still effective?

If it was the other person who made you feel this way, what was he like? Are any of his or her actions something you can emulate?

Answering these and other questions will help you identify your social strengths and weaknesses. Take apart the previous interactions you've had and try to break down these situations guided by the concepts introduced within this chapter.

If you are not able to answer these questions by yourself, it can help to find a person you trust who can be honest and objective with you.

Once you've chosen a person who can discuss these things with you, remind yourself to always look at the goals of this process so that you can be more receptive even when you hear difficult things about yourself. Always, always look at this as a task you are doing to allow yourself to improve socially and do better in the future.

Another good thing to do is to list down your answers to these questions. It can be very challenging to have a full understanding of one's self. It is a long process and it can be easy to get lost in all the new things you may not have been previously aware of.

This is the time to take a look at the good, the bad, and the ugly in you. Your pride may be the most sensitive issue in this process. It will be a very humbling experience so start telling yourself that everything will be okay. Do not focus on the pain this might cause your ego; focus on the benefits of having better social outcomes in the future instead.

Raising your social IQ will require you to see how you stack up against everybody else. The most effective way of approaching this is to have a good sense of self-awareness.

Please do not confuse this with being self-conscious, though. Being self-aware means you can identify your strengths and weaknesses without other people having to call you out on them. Being self-conscious on the other hand is when you are constantly being too critical of yourself and you end up letting it take over your process.

Self-awareness should lead to the discovery and better management of your strengths and weaknesses. It should not take you to the path of self-destruction. Being aware of your strengths will not only give you confidence. It will also allow you to offer your capabilities to others. Having an understanding of your weaknesses is beneficial to help you avoid making the same mistakes you've made before.

The biggest mistake you will ever make if you're just starting to learn about social intelligence is prioritizing other people's issues. Remember, if there's one thing you are sure to have control over, it is yourself. Even if you have difficult habits to break, you will still find it easier to manage your own nasty habits than the habits of those other than you.

The bottom line is: it all starts with you.

2

SOCIAL ASSETS AND LIABILITIES

Once you get a detailed view of your social tendencies, it's time for you to learn how to plot out your social assets and liabilities. Now that you have a better look at how social exchanges work, you must now know how these interactions tend to lead to more events as well.

For example, you are at a party and you start telling everyone about your break up with your significant other. Many of these people will feel sorry for you and will respond kindly with supportive words and gestures.

Some of them may also have had individual issues that they were dealing with at the time you were announcing your epic breakup to everyone. These people would rather not focus on your romantic issues simply because they don't have the energy for it and have no interest whatsoever in this personal matter you are talking about. These people are potential friends, business partners, or clients.

Since you have shared this information with them, most of them have started avoiding you in fear of not having the right words to say to you. To them, you are now "The Breakup Guy".

This doesn't sound like such a bad thing but is that what you really want to be labeled as?

Over the next few days, weeks, months, or maybe even years, you have completely moved on from this but the other people have already marked you as this person who had nothing else to talk about but his failed relationship. Some of these people may only have this as a reference for you in their head if no other more significant conversations between you and them occurred after.

At that party, one person there could have become your friend. You both love this Mexican restaurant down the road and you always ordered the same chicken quesadilla from their menu. Unfortunately, when this person sat beside you, you asked her why women just can't understand you and they all end up leaving you. It didn't have to be in the messy, dramatic manner you see actors do in movies.

You could have said this however way you wanted. The point is, you had that moment wherein you could have started a friendship with someone. But instead of that, this person ended up too alienated by a strong sentiment you have that she had zero background with.

And nope, giving her a detailed background is not enough to lure her into your breakup story. In fact, it might even drive her further away from you. This person was not a part of the romantic relationship you had with your previous significant other. There is no way for her to participate appropriately in this narrative you are sharing with her. Nowhere in this situation will she be able to find something to share with you.

Before you start a conversation, think about what you and the other person will gain for it. It can be humor, wisdom, or support. Whatever it is, conversations are supposed to be a two-way street so you have to consider what both parties will be taking away from this encounter.

Think clearly about the consequences and what value it will have to the person you are sharing this moment with. Time and energy are spent whenever you are engaging in social interaction. If you make it worthwhile for both you and the other party, everybody wins and people will be more drawn to you.

Aside from oversharing, another way of creating social liabilities is not being careful about sensitive topics. Some information can lead to people being hurt and companies being negatively affected. Again, it is better to assess what value the information you transfer will have to the other person. Is it worth the responsibilities afterward?

Your boss will not be happy if he finds out you spilled vital information about your company to others. Your spouse will get embarrassed if you talk about how he or she has smelly socks to people you do not even know well. Your client will not be impressed if he catches you making fun of his accent in front of other people.

Anything you say or do can affect the reputation and the relationships you build. The clearer your understanding of how you come off in social situations, the more guided your choices will be.

A person's reputation is formed from a collection of his previous words and actions while a relationship is built from a collection of previous experiences and interactions with another person. What if you have separate books for your reputation and each of your relationships? These books will automatically log everything you say and do.

Will you enjoy the things written about you? Do you admire this person and is this the person you aspire to be? Think carefully about these things. It may not be logged in imaginary books but the people you interact with will have memories of these interactions with you.

If you have social liabilities, you also have your social assets. These are the qualities that are unique to you and what attracts people to you.

To find out what your social assets are, you have to put yourself in a serious self-assessment once more. What draws people closer to you? What drives them away from you? Once you get a full grasp of these things, it will be easier for you to tweak the way you approach conversations, transactions, and even public speaking.

Try to think about the people you like spending time and conversing with. What makes you trust them? What makes having moments with them enjoyable? Now reverse this question. Ask yourself what people admire about you.

If you have great humor, people will go to you because they enjoy fun conversations with you. If you are a good planner, people will go to you for strategic advice. Some people have the gift of warmth, they can give emotional relief to troubled people. If you are one of them, then this is also an asset that you can add to your personal brand.

It will also be very helpful to find this out through the people you interact with. Find time to talk about your hesitations and questions with those you trust. It can be your boss, a good friend, or your family.

Ask your spouse or your parents when they enjoy your company the most. Take a look at how your boss responds to the things you say or do. If your boss is open to it, you may even ask them about it. These are what employee assessments are for. Take advantage of these assessments so you can use them to better your social skills.

Choose people you can listen to. This may be challenging at first. It is understandable to feel self-conscious when you ask people about yourself. If you choose the right people in your life, they will under-stand and they may even appreciate the fact that you are humbling yourself so that you can make improve-ments in your life. Those who truly care about you will most likely be supportive of this.

If making you aware of your social liabilities can help you foster relationships better, it's the same with finding out what your social assets are. Think of them as the currency you use to create connections with other people.

Remember to always see social engagements as an exchange. You can't really get people to want to be with you and work with you if they do not appreciate anything in your company, right?

It is not that people require things before they start building relationships with you. It is not about you. It is about the way you make them feel, the things they learn from you, and the things they get to share with you. Will you spend time with someone who makes you feel uncomfortable? Will you remember someone who you cannot have enjoyable or meaningful experiences with?

3

PRACTICE BEING AUTHENTIC

I am sure you have heard of this before. Your personal brand is basically the compilation of you, your unique qualities, the things you aim for, and all the other things that make up the life that you want and the person you want to be.

So how is it different from your social assets?

Your social assets are the things you are good at. They are basically your main features and your selling point. It's what you have that makes people remember you and connect with you.

A personal brand, however, does not necessarily have to make considerations for what people want from you. It is looking beyond the requirements of others and knowing what makes you feel like your authentic self. There is no other way for you to figure out your personal brand other than honest self-discovery.

We have learned about this earlier as a means to understand yourself and your social tendencies. This time, though, we will use introspection as a means to get to know your personal priorities and source of happiness.

But first, why is this essential in gaining social intelligence?

For others to feel a connection and trust with us, we must strive to be more authentic. Have you ever felt uncomfortable with someone before and you got a hunch that this person was not being sincere towards you?

That may seem like a presumptuous thought to have but the truth is people do instinctively feel it when someone is not being truthful. If you experience it, others do too. If there was ever a time when you were not being yourself, there might have been a chance the other person felt it and he reacted in some way. Try and look back if this has ever happened to you and try to look at the cues you may have missed at that time.

No one likes to be deceived.

Lying is, of course, immoral. In philosophy, lying is bad because it is considered as a misuse of language which is essential to human societies. Language is a form of contract or commitment. When people lie, it is a commitment to a word that is not even true therefore those who have received lies are misled into something that is unjust.

Lying diminishes trust in any kind of relationship. Take note of the word that was used to describe language –commitment. Whenever you speak of something untrue, you are committing to this information. Lies are exhausting to protect and once they are exposed, it is likely impossible to rebuild the trust that was lost.

When you lie, you have to backtrack on all the things you said that day and you have to stick to them in the future. If this is a habit to you, the harder it is to cover up the holes in your story. Eventually, people may catch up to you and you are exposed when you least expect it. Do you realize just how tiring that can be?

Another reason why being authentic to your personal brand is important is that when you stand alongside other people, the only thing that makes you interesting and sets you apart from everybody else is actually your genuine self and no other. This is the only thing that is yours and no one else can take it away from you but you yourself.

Your personal brand is what guides you to stay true to your authentic self. It is easy to get lost in all the things that are happening in our lives especially today when we are exposed to a lot of different influences.

With the speed of globalization and the large presence of social media in our lives, it has become harder than ever to get to know our true selves. The way we value relationships, the people we aspire to be, and our very own self-worth is greatly affected by the orientation we get from a wide variety of sources.

The thing with being authentic is that you can only find it within yourself. You cannot follow someone else's path if it does not resonate with you.

Imagine a jigsaw puzzle. You are given an assortment of puzzle pieces. Some of them are meant to fit your full picture and some of them belong to a different puzzle set. This is what it's like in the world today.

Not all the things you are exposed to match your personal brand. There is no way for you to accommodate everything.

In a puzzle, what happens to the full picture if you try and fit mismatched pieces together?

First, you will get frustrated. You try your best to force the pieces together and they just would not fit with each other. They may not even be in the same size range so you might even damage the puzzle pieces as you aggressively attach them to the other tiles.

Second, you have a harder time getting started and getting finished. You have an assortment of pieces that don't necessarily belong together. If you do not take a look at the pieces and start to get rid of those that don't match, you will keep going back and forth and get lost in a loop of confusion.

Your time and energy are wasted and there's a chance you may never even get to finish the puzzle.

Lastly, nobody gets the whole picture. The main goal of building a puzzle is to end up with an actual full image. Because you wanted to include pieces that did not belong to your set, you now have a distorted final output that people have a hard time understanding.

You end up with an uneven, unnatural picture that no one gets the point of.

That's what happens to your self-image if you try and force yourself to accommodate all the influences you see. You will just end up frustrated with your energy wasted. There is nothing more tiring than forcing yourself to be someone you are not at peace to be. Your time and effort are being depleted but you only get a distorted version of yourself in the end.

We can also liken this process to wearing a mask. The mask works in two ways, it hides what's underneath it and it allows you to portray a certain persona on the outside. It can be anything that you can think of. It can even be a replica of your real image.

Most people have a tendency to curate how they present themselves to others with the goal of portraying what they think the best image of themself is. However, the person places his or herself in a situation where his genuine personality and self-image are being compromised in the process of doing so. This affects a person's self-esteem and happiness.

The caveat with masks is that although you get to hide your identity, it doesn't actually erase your true self. What you're only doing is pushing it back down but it's still spilling out of you and everyone else in front of you just sees a watered-down version between the real you and the person you're pretending to be.

The key thing is you're exerting effort to actually bury your genuine self and pretend to be this ideal you have inside of your head. There even comes a point when you are no longer able to tell whether you're still pretending or not.

Oftentimes, people put on masks because they are not comfortable with the idea they have of themselves. It is not always because they are ashamed of their true selves.

One, it could be because they have never tried to show their true colors before and they are afraid that others will not like the real them very much. This is a fear of failure.

Two, it is a good excuse to risk mistakes. There are people who find it hard to admit to their misgivings. Sometimes it's about pride, at times it is a fear of accountability. Since the real identity is hidden, there's suddenly no responsibility or liability. The disguise fools you into thinking that anything you say or do while you're wearing the mask won't put the real you in danger.

This system can create two different paths for you. One is you slowly become the person you are pretending to be and all is well and good for you. The other is that you eventually are not able to catch up with these different personas and your mask slowly disintegrates and the real person is revealed.

The connections we make and the trust we build

with others rely almost entirely on the person we show ourselves to be in front of other people.

Being able to establish a personal brand that is authentic to you will help you manage and invest your time and energy in the right social situations. It also helps you connect with people better because they feel your sincerity and they see your consistency.

However, being authentic is not always easy for many people. Most people don't even see when they are being inauthentic.

It takes a lot of courage, humility, and introspection to be able to identify when you are truly yourself. Being authentic does not only involve who your genuine self is. It also includes knowing who you want to be and who you never want to be.

Here are a few steps you can take to practice being authentic:

1. INCREASE YOUR SELF-AWARENESS

Masks are an easy go-to for a lot of people. Do not worry, you are not the only one wearing a mask and neither are you being condemned for even wearing one.

Masks are not always a bad thing. When you are

in the workplace, you have a persona that you try to maintain because it keeps everything in order. You get to focus more and you are in keeping with the professional atmosphere because you respect your colleagues and the environment you are in. This is a way for people to adapt and do well in a given situation.

However, there are masks that are unnecessary and can be used for destructive purposes. One example is spending beyond your means to dress up your social status. This will be a cycle that never ends well.

The important thing is that you recognize the masks you wear and you know when and where it starts and ends. This requires a great sense of self-awareness which you can achieve through introspection.

Think about the masks you wear and your reasons for doing so. Identify whether these masks are in conflict with your personal brand and never confuse them for your genuine self.

2. AVOID FILTERS AS MUCH AS POSSIBLE

Being your raw, authentic self is not always easy especially when you are in an unfamiliar environment. Because of this, you feel the need to stay in your bubble to protect yourself from scrutiny. All of us have fears and insecurities but it is okay to be vulnerable sometimes. The only way for you to find your true self and establish your personal brand is by taking risks.

Engage in raw interactions with different people and observe how they respond to you. Most of the time, this will result in the same courtesy coming from them. You will start to notice that people are more relaxed and comfortable to be real around you, too. You connect with them more and the gestures you share become more sincere and authentic.

When you are sincere, the other party catches on and there is a sense of trust that is built between the two of you. You will be able to tell when the other person becomes more at ease with you.

The more you practice this, the more you realize when you are most comfortable being yourself too. When your sincere actions are validated and recipro-cated, you are more encouraged to take this approach in future situations.

This is not to say that you will no longer make adjustments to accommodate the person in front of you. There is still a difference between talking to someone you work with and your childhood friend.

You always have to keep going back to your social liabilities. Being raw does not mean you get rid of all formalities you practice to make others feel more comfortable around you.

Learn to improvise and be more in touch with your intuition so you can navigate your way towards authenticity without being tactless or arrogant. This way you get to overcome your hesitations and self-doubt.

3. BE HONEST

Authenticity will always include honesty for reasons that are obvious. Lying should never be a constant routine in your life. This will only lead to a dangerous cycle and people are guaranteed to catch on sooner or later.

Risking the loss of trust and confidence of the people around you will just make things more complicated and will require even more effort from you.

This is not to say that you have to be brutally honest about everything. If your significant other makes you breakfast and she burns the toast, the usual reaction is to say "It's okay". Even when you are already late for your job and you are hungrier than a lion, you say this because it is not worth upsetting your partner with.

What you have to see is the intention behind your lie. Lying about your thoughts on burnt toast is totally different from lying about owning an expensive car. What thoughts will the person you are lying to have after you share false information with them? Who is affected by the lies you are speaking? Why do you even have to lie to begin with?

Ask yourself these questions first if you feel the need to lie.

4. JEALOUSY CAN GET THE BEST OUT OF YOU

Your best friend has his own house, a new car, a beautiful girlfriend, is successful in his career, and on top of it, he is stylish and handsome. You aspire for all of these things for yourself because you see that he has it all. What do you do?

It is not bad to be motivated and to work hard to achieve and get great things for yourself. What is bad is when your standards come from the accomplishments of others. Your best friend acquired those things not because he wanted to compete with you.

He achieved those things to better himself. That is what you also need to do.

It is the saddest thing when a person bases his happiness and fulfillment from how he compares to others. If you want a new car, get it. If you want your own house, get it. But think very well about what these things are for.

Chasing the standards of others is an endless road. You can never be truly fulfilled because you always look at what others have accomplished around you instead of your own victories.

There will always be someone better than you in some ways. This does not make you any less of a person. What is important is that you know who you are and you strive to be better at the things you sincerely want.

When you see other people getting the things you wanted for yourself as well, work hard for it but never ask yourself why they were able to get it before you did. Every person has his own obstacles to overcome.

Do not mistake greed for goals.

5. LEARN TO PROCESS FEEDBACK

Feedback is not something you should be wary of. In fact, feedback should be valued. When a person reacts to you and tells you how your behavior affects them, the first thing you should do is listen.

You do this not just because you want to please that person. You do this because you want to get to know yourself even more and how you come across to other people.

It is possible that your words and your gestures do not always represent your authentic self at times. Learn from this feedback so that you can better and more effectively communicate your true self to others.

Your actions after finding out how people react to your behavior are completely yours to decide on. Make sure it still fits with your personal brand and the person you aspire to be. This exercise is meant to empower you to make better choices in the future.

After getting feedback, avoid making excuses for yourself. If this is you come off to other people, that is your responsibility. Yes, others can be wrong about you at times but it is better to know why and how you make these impressions to them.

Making excuses and admitting to your mistakes

are both habit-forming actions. If making excuses becomes a habit to you, it will be hard for you to realize when you are wrong. This prevents you from making positive adjustments to yourself. However, if admitting to your mistakes is the habit you choose, you are always given the chance to really learn from your mistakes and acknowledge the changes you have to make. Which habit will you choose?

6. ALLOW YOURSELF TO CHANGE

Think of authenticity as a goal that you have for yourself. It is not an innate quality that naturally comes out of people. A part of being authentic is accepting that no one is perfect. Mistakes and self-doubt are completely natural.

Allow yourself to make the most out of this journey. If you have committed mistakes in the past, make peace with it, and figure out where to adjust.

Stop worrying about feeling small and being ridiculed for your flaws. You are defined by your actions and not what others think or say about you. It is what you do afterward that matters.

If your mistakes are really bothering you, just think of it this way, you are now aware of the things you did wrong. There is no possible way for you to turn back time and do things differently at that moment. You can only move forward.

But, unlike before, you are now aware of the consequences of your actions. The best way to make up for your mistakes is to try your best not to repeat them again. Do not let shame get in the way of your self-improvement. Take this as an opportunity and be serious about doing better after this.

4

STOP TRYING TO GET EVERYONE'S STOP

*P*robably the biggest hurdle when it comes to being authentic and sticking to your personal brand is when you start trying to get other people's approval. That said, it can keep you further away from improving your social intelligence.

Trying to get everyone's approval is a big problem. The hardest part about it is that it is perfectly natural to feel like you have to get on everybody's good side to be able to socialize gracefully.

Wanting to feel loved, needed, smart, and attractive are all indications of a person's need for approval. These are all-natural and it's perfectly human to want to be accepted.

In fact, this is something that's found in nature itself. Peacocks spread their colorfully patterned feathers to attract a potential mate. Birds of paradise use dance as a mating ritual to invite a prospective partner. Baboons form cliques based on the personality of their peers.

We humans have our version of such practices. It is ingrained in our nature to feel as though we need to be accepted to be able to thrive and survive.

When I was in elementary school, I had two mates that I spent most of my time after school with. We take lunch breaks together. We get out of class together and head to this one guy's, let's call him Gary's, home. I was a bit of a math, language, and science geek and the three of us will spend our time studying and conversing about such things together.

A couple of years later, one of the popular kids in school started being buddies with me. We got along and soon enough I was part of the cool pack in our school. It happened quickly and I never noticed my departure from my group with Gary. I just started not hanging out with them anymore.

It was great to be with the "it" crowd. We had our own table in the cafeteria and we always had someplace to go to. It felt really great to be worthy of this spot in the group.

A year into this new group I am now a part of, I no longer spent time away from school reading about science and math. In fact, my grades started to plummet. Well, I had A's so it was not really a big deal. I was not failing any of my classes. It did not look like my life was getting ruined. I hung out with them until high school.

The first year of high school was exciting. My group was getting more popular than ever. We would go out every day after school. We eat out, go to the hippest places, and keep up with the latest trends back then.

And then there was one small issue. I did not have enough money to keep up with our lifestyle. I started not going to the usual cool places with them. Instead of going out, I started getting interested in the stuff I liked before. I started reading again. I spent more time at home and in the library compared to hanging out with my clique.

Because I was immersing myself in all of these things, it was spilling out of me and the excitement of sharing my interests with my mates grew. I would talk about the glories of math, science, and nature with my clique. Unfortunately, it just was not interesting to them. At times they would flat out laugh at my face because I sounded like a nerd to them like it was such a comical thing to be.

Honestly, there were times I bought into it. I

asked myself why I was going back to this childhood interest of mine that I had already gotten rid of. Whenever I felt I was being ridiculed, I would find ways to get another dose of coolness. Money was still an issue and I started feeling like I had to get the money to be able to hang out with them again so that I could go back to being the cool guy they preferred.

One day, I was walking towards our lunch table in school and my mates completely ignored me and walked out of the cafeteria. It was embarrassing and I thought maybe I was just being too sensitive about it. Maybe they were just done with lunch and had somewhere else to be. The same thing happened everywhere I followed them too.

I felt so small. Yet, the smaller I felt, the more I had to chase after them. I just had to be in the group again and it was my fault because I started boring them. I needed to do something, anything to get my friends back.

I never did. I finished high school, went through college, and started working without my "cool" friends with me. This incident left a bitter taste in my tongue and I never had a group again. I had friends but I never hung out with the same people constantly. It was traumatizing to me and I figured all people are like that.

The cool guys continued to be friends with each other over the years. With the age of social media, it became an annoying thing to see them together and grow up as close friends. Admittedly, it still pisses me off when I see them post pictures of their parties and get-togethers. I feel bad when I see them happy together with their wives and kids.

I felt shamed by these people and in my head, I wished the group falls apart and I would be vindicated from the injustice of being abandoned by them.

Then one day, my old friend Gary contacted me. He brought along our third friend and we had drinks after work. It was like nothing changed between the three of us. We shared our love for our old interests and new interests were explored as well. We had a great time.

Over the course of this meeting, how I left the group was brought up. They were not angry with me or anything. They just said it was surprising to them that I was no longer spending time with them.

I tried to look back on it and I honestly did not think I was leaving my two friends behind. I just thought I was with new friends that I enjoyed more. And that's what they thought too.

They told me they felt bad when they witnessed

how I started losing my new friends and that they saw how that experience had transformed me. Although they felt sorry for me, we were all kids and we simply did not know how to approach the situation back then. We all moved forward and now we're here.

No, this was not a prodigal son story of me getting back into the group once more. But, meeting with them showed me how easy it is to lose sight of your own self when you get into a mindset of chasing other people's approval. Regret is something I have learned to manage and I can honestly say it is not worth dwelling on things like that. However, the lessons gathered from that experience should never be erased.

All the things I did to chase the approval of others were exhausting mentally, physically, financially, and emotionally. But when I look back on it, I did not have to go through all of that if I had just realized what really made me happy at that time.

I had two friends all along that I shared my love for the things that piqued my interest. This is not to say that I should not have been friends with anybody else but them. The point is I lost myself because I favored someone else's idea of a better me.

We can continue to thrive even if we maintain

our own personal brands. We were all kids back then but the "cool kids" may have seen through me back then. I was not myself anymore and I was already struggling with my own pretensions.

I cringe at the thought of my old self back then. I said things to keep them interested. I bought things that did not really matter to me but were a thing to them. I hung out with them even though I no longer felt like it and that took my energy away from the things I actually liked.

The trick with the human mind is: non-acceptance is equal to rejection. This burdens us so much and it pushes us to place our energies in the things that frustrate us.

Because I am the lead in my story, it looks like I was bullied and the "cool kids" rejected me. However, take a look at my trio with Gary. I did the same thing to them but it never actually bothered me. In all honesty, I did not think much of the abandonment I did. I was simply moving forward.

And that was it. It took years for me to realize that we had different interests and it was not always about making me feel bad. The very fact that no matter what I did I never really connected with them again shows that it was not about getting favors from me. My brand no longer fits theirs.

Looking at it that way makes it easier to understand. It is not always like how it is portrayed in movies. I never thought of Gary as a bad, boring guy. That thought never crossed my mind. It was never personal.

Gary had the right perspective on things. He knew me and he knew it was not about him. He never chased me. He never spoke badly about the "cool kids" just to get on my good side.

Gary went on and continued to be Gary. One day, he felt like talking to me again so he made the call and we hung out.

Meanwhile, I was drenched in self-pity and self-doubt. Honestly, I am so used to being bitter about the other group and I still would not get myself to be casual with them again.

The feeling of rejection has a good way of killing your self-esteem. You are convinced that you are the opposite of the things you aspire to be. You are not loved. You are not needed. You are dumb. You are ugly. These feelings start to consume you. Suddenly, you become this distrustful, hateful person who finds it impossible to see others happy.

In a study, researchers found that rejection induces the same response in the brain as physical pain. Another study shows that all but 2 of 15 school shooters were rejected. Rejection causes a yearning for retaliation and closing off in a person's brain.

Gary has thought me a precious lesson that I am lucky to have received. The feeling of rejection starts with how you interpret the differences you have with other people.

I was not all that bad as a kid, though. I got something right.

I am very fortunate to have a close relationship with my parents. During those tumultuous times in my youth, I had them to talk to. However, I found one of their responses to be ridiculous.

My father told me that the reason I was being rejected was that I was starting to look like a threat. My peers were not very happy to be friends with someone who had the mind to accommodate valuable knowledge and this seems like something they could not achieve for themselves. They did not like me because I was better than them

It was not the idea that they were jealous that sounded ridiculous to me and it could have been true as well. What I found ridiculous was the idea that I was the focus of their behavior and that they think I am better than them.

This is ridiculous because it will send me on another destructive path. I did not think I had to be better than them. I did not like the idea of lifting myself up for them. It just felt unnatural to me.

Back then I didn't know why I felt that way. Now that I am older, I realize that there is no need for me to be better than them for them to hate on me. Those feelings of jealousy that they had, it was not on me. Even if I do tons better than them or so much worse than them, it does not matter.

I cannot solve their own insecurities and thinking that I am better than them will not solve my insecurities as well. The best way to look at it is that we just did not click anymore. It was nobody's fault. Dealing with these things should be met with a lot more kindness but not everyone has that capacity and expecting that from everyone will only break your heart. Always remember that it is not always personal.

There is also no point in convincing yourself that you are better than those who you feel rejected you. What matters is your genuine self. You are a completely separate entity from them and if you have done all that you can that is in keeping with your personal brand, it is no longer your battle to fight.

Some people will never like you and there are people you will never like too. That's just how life is.

Do not worry about other people's approval. Your approval of your own self and happiness is the one that counts the most.

Is this the life that you want? What do you need to do to get the life that you want? Focus on that and let others be.

At the end of the day, if the people you spend time with and the actions you make do not fit your aspirations and your values, then you will never find fulfillment and happiness.

5

IMPROVE YOUR COMMUNICATION SKILLS

*N*ow, it's time to focus on communicating with others. A book on social intelligence will not make sense if it does not address the way you communicate your inner thoughts and needs.

The very reason why humans are capable of gaining social intelligence is that they have the capacity of interacting and being understood by others. This is how we are able to form relationships and participate in social organizations.

Communication plays a big role in improving your social intelligence and effective communication may mean the difference between a successful and a failed social relationship.

At this point in the book, you may have gotten to know yourself better. This is the most essential thing to learn before you work on improving your communication skills. That's the very reason why we spent the first few chapters trying to understand your inner self first.

If you do not know yourself well enough, there is no way for you to express your feelings and ideas clearly. Once you have a firm understanding of yourself that is when you are ready to plot your way towards good and effective communication.

It is like trying to cook a stew without having all the ingredients first. You are halfway into cooking and then you realize you need something that's missing from your pantry but you go ahead with it anyway. What happens then? You do not get the best out of your dish. It may not even taste the way you intended it to be and the regret sets in.

Since you now know the steps to get a full view of yourself. We will now delve into the importance of communicating yourself to others well.

The heart of social interactions is effective communication. It is very important to improve your communication skills if you want to develop your social intelligence.

Notice how we say effective communication and

not just communication alone? It is because anyone can communicate. You can communicate all you want, as often as you would like, and as loudly as you can but your message and intention never completely come through. Even if the other person hears you, he or she may not fully understand what you are trying to communicate. Or worse, the person might end up misinterpreting you.

Instead of being able to get your point across, you get into this frustrating exchange that ends up as a waste of time and energy.

So, how do you improve your communication?

To be able to communicate competently, you have to first develop what is called verbal fluency. Verbal fluency enables a person to articulate his or her ideas freely without strain.

A way to better understand verbal fluency is to compare it to dancing. To improve your dancing skills, you must develop your reflexes and muscles well. As you work on your reflexes and muscle strength, dancing becomes much easier. You will get better at executing the dance steps once you master these two things. Dancing becomes an instinct to you and you are able to do more difficult moves with less effort.

That's what it's like to have strong verbal

fluency. As you practice good communication more and more, the better you are able to articulate yourself with less effort.

If you use steps in dancing, you use language in communication. Your verbal fluency determines how well you are able to use language in communication. Once verbal fluency is harnessed, language becomes instinctive to you to and you will be able to manage your energy better when you are engaging in social interaction.

The thing with language is that it is actually a combination of your verbal and non-verbal expressions. People often constrain language to words and that is why there are people who say all the right words without getting their intended responses.

Body language is an important part of communication. You can communicate a lot of things even without the use of words.

Take babies for example. There is no other way for them to express happiness, sadness, and frustration but through their facial expressions and body gestures. Yet, you understand them.

This is also the reason why people who do not share the same verbal language get to somehow communicate. You must take note of the gestures you make and the practices you have whenever you are trying to interact with someone.

Take a look at your habits as well. For example, when you are doing public speaking, too much movement can become distracting to your audience. This may also be caused by a lack of confidence. When people are unsure of the way they say things and the words that they speak, the body turns to fidgeting.

Body language says a ton about a person, perhaps even more than verbal communication. It's one of the toughest things to control and it is hard to restrain.

Another non-verbal you can use is to maintain eye contact. By maintaining eye contact, you lock your audience in. You appear confident and assertive so you do not lose their attention. It also shows commitment so your audience tries to listen more closely to you.

Space is also a non-verbal that people usually forget about. If you get too close to a person during a confrontation, you might make them feel uncomfortable. The other person may take this as an intrusion in their personal space and he ends up focusing on closing off from you.

Even the way you are dressed is considered non-verbal language. If you are dressed down, this sends a message that you are casual. In a business setting, this may not be the best thing. If you also dress up too formally for a casual event, it may not match the relaxed atmosphere and people may get intimidated by this.

Non-verbal language also includes voice –not statements, but a voice. Your audience reads into the timing and pacing of your words, the dynamics or loudness and softness of your voice, your tone, and inflections.

You have to be aware of these things because your audience gets signals and give meaning to these things, too. The changes you make to any of these elements can affect the way your audience responds to you.

Meanwhile, being in close proximity to the person you are talking to can also be a signal for trust and intimacy if such a precedent is established early on in the interaction.

The best way to avoid unnecessary and mismatched non-verbal is to become self-aware. Try and practice talking in front of the mirror and notice if what you are saying matches the gestures you make. No one will ever believe you if you say you are happy yet your face is upside down and you are wailing your lungs out.

You can also get yourself a partner who can critique the way you move as you converse. Ask them for feedback and take note of both the things you do well in and the things you have to improve on. Finding out about your good points can help you improve your confidence further too.

Now we go to the traditional form of language which is verbal language. This is, of course, an essential part of human interaction and a huge part of social intelligence.

The most important thing you have to practice in verbal communication is clarity. The first mistake of people who aspire to be good speakers is that they decorate their speech too much with unnecessary words. They focus too much on sounding smart versus being understood.

To be understood, you have to be clear and to the point. There is no need to clutter your messages with flowery words and pointless jargon. Use simple English as much as possible so that your audience can focus more on your statement and less effort is needed just to try and decode whatever it is you are trying to say. If you find yourself using intricate language and giving unnecessary details to pad your perceived insecurities, stop and take a moment to adjust your language.

Make it your goal to be able to articulate your statements as concisely as possible. Conversations are not a competition in the number of words you can come up with. When it comes to effective communication, quality is preferred over quantity.

You have a problem if you are more comfortable saying, "My myocardium, the scientific word for heart, is experiencing some sort of suffering because I have not been able to see you for a very long time." Versus, "I miss you".

Always start conversations with intent. Do not tire your audience before you even land your point. Beating around the bush is not helpful to anyone. It only depletes time and energy.

When you start conversations with your main statement, your audience is guided properly in the conversation and you both spend your time and energy entertaining more valid points.

Beating around the bush is also a sign of self-doubt and lack of confidence. You are only fooling yourself if you keep dragging your speech because you are unsure of your statement. You will only end up confusing your audience and this is the last thing you want if your goal is to communicate effectively.

Lastly, the best approach to language is to just be

simple and straightforward in your communication. Take it easy and do not let your jitters get the best of you. Always go back to who you are and what your priorities are so that you can maintain being upfront and clear whenever you try to communicate.

6

COMMUNICATE LIKE YOUR LIFE
DEPENDS ON IT

*T*here are a number of things we use communication for. Communication is used to share information, give opinions, ask questions, express our desires and needs, participate socially, and many more. A lot of devices and systems are created just so that people are able to communicate.

According to Marco Polo, Genghis Khan had horse riders pass messages between stations 25 miles apart. This system allowed messages to be delivered as far as 300 miles a day and some attribute the success of his empire to this communication system.

Can you imagine the world without cellphones and the internet today? If airplanes did not have a communication system, traveling by air would become dangerous. Having an emergency hotline line like 911 can save lives. Because it is so essential to our lives, opportunities for communication are created every day.

In the previous chapter, we discussed how to communicate effectively. Now we will talk about when and why it is important to communicate. There is no other way for people to understand you and for you to get through to anyone without communication. Having the right tools to communicate is pointless if you do not use them for the right purposes.

Communication is what you have to invest in interpersonal relationships. Without it, there is no way for you to build anything with anyone. Transactions are a form of communication. Chitchatting is communication. Teaching is communication. A smile, a hug, a kiss are expressions that communicate.

In the workplace, the system will break down if even a small amount of information is left out. Say a client has emailed a proposal to you and it does not reach the department it intends to communicate with. The proposal never gets to you. Nothing happens and the deal will never exist.

Besides the need to exchange information, we are also able to influence others through communication. What we say and do can affect other people in many ways. It can motivate, strengthen, and build relationships. It can change a person's mindset, encourage him, and it can also bring relief to a person who is struggling.

Mental health is an issue many people are struggling with and sometimes being able to communicate is what makes the right impact in a person's condition. There are people who are not able to express their hopelessness and fears but once they start receiving the right motivation and relief, their whole outlook in life changes.

That is what communication can do all you have to do is learn when and how you should use it.

So how can you apply communication in a social setting?

1. A SMILE GOES A LONG WAY

The simple gesture creates an endless ripple effect. When you get to the office and your coworkers greet you with a smile, it changes your mood and demeanor. You respond with a smile and start greeting everyone else with a smile too. Everyone ends up smiling. And then, one coworker arrives late with an angry look in his face. You all begin to be bothered by this person. You say hi to him with a pleasant and sincere grin. Instead of responding nicely to you, this person does not even look at you. How would this make you feel?

Even your facial expression can send signals to the people around you. Be aware of your nonverbal and adjust it according to the effect you want on people.

2. MAKE FRIENDS

Get to know people by talking about yourself and listening to their stories too. Do not hesitate to open up to people as long as it is in the right context of the situation you are in. If it is just a casual chat, talk about your interests lightly, and let the conversation progress.

Small interactions can lead to deeper relationships too. It all depends on the amount of investment you put into the relationship. Just remember to keep your social liabilities in mind and be authentic with your communication.

3. BE VULNERABLE SOMETIMES

Oftentimes, people are afraid of communication because of insecurities stemming from inexperience and previous trauma. Do not let this get in the way of connecting to people. Mistakes are mistakes. The most important thing is that you recognize them, move forward, and adjust.

Insecurities and mistakes can be sources of motivation as well. When you start to talk about your fears and worries, other people are given the opportunity to help you with them and also to learn from them.

It is also a way for leaders to encourage growth and become more approachable. When leaders are open to talk about mistakes, it builds trust and confidence within their team. The other team members are more comfortable asking for guidance and they are also more at ease at recognizing and adjusting their mistakes.

4. TELL STORIES

Stories can have a lot of influence on people. They can get motivation, hope, and confidence just by listening to powerful stories that resonate with them.

The stories do not have to be complicated and lengthy. As long as they carry great lessons and relatable situations, they can impact the lives of other people and sometimes even communities.

This is why the stories of great people are told and they continue to fascinate and motivate people around the world. The stories of great leaders, heroes, and other inspiring icons. These stories affect the lives of many.

5. ACKNOWLEDGE THE GOOD IN PEOPLE

Tell people what you appreciate about them. Do not hesitate to compliment someone for a job well done or for any good deed, small or big. It gives positive motivation and it gives confidence to people.

Think about the time you were thanked for something? How did it make you feel? Pay a positive experience forward. People will be encouraged to do good when they are recognized for the good things they do.

6. TELL PEOPLE WHAT YOU NEED

If you want to spend time with someone, tell them. If you need space, say it. If you need more direction, ask for it. When something offends you, confront it. Even babies try to communicate when they are hungry or need a diaper change.

Not being able to tell people what you need only creates animosity for you and confusion to others. It is your responsibility to let people know what you need. You should not expect everyone to automatically know how you feel and where your discomforts are coming from.

Find a proper place and time for it then discuss it with the other person with clarity and respect. Do not be passive-aggressive about it. As long as you are dealing with a sensible person and you are respectful with your request, the other person will discuss things with you in the proper manner.

7. ASK QUESTIONS

Do not hesitate to ask about things you are interested in and the things you want to learn from. Just make sure to ask respectfully and ask at the right place and at the right time. You can learn a lot from other people. Sometimes you even think you know about something fully well but hearing about it from other people shows you what you missed.

8. RESPOND TO PEOPLE

When you receive a message, acknowledge receipt and respond appropriately. If someone sends you a lengthy, informative message, try to reciprocate the effort that remains within the context of your conversation. Remember to keep it concise and sincere, though.

When you get an email that is detailed and helpful to you, you cannot just respond with "K". Thank the person, acknowledge how it is helpful, and do it quickly.

Delaying your response will only risk forgetting about it. Also, when you delay a response, the other person may think you either have not received their message or the message was not received well.

9. THANK PEOPLE

Acknowledge people when they offer ideas and suggestions. Say thank you when you are given an update or a heads up.

When you ignore these gestures, people will think their actions were unhelpful and unappreciated. This sends a bad cue to your peer especially if their input was requested. They will stop connecting with you and, worse, they might even get offended by your lack of response.

Thanking people will also motivate them to help you out even more. When people see that they are helping and that they are recognized for their efforts, they are more willing to do more to help you.

There are many other situations that will require effective communication from you. It will all depend on your goals and intentions. Just remember these few important things to guide you through.

Practice so that you will gain courage and confidence.

Be respectful so that people will respect you too.

Be sensitive about other people's needs and comforts.

Know the right timing.

Be clear with your communication.

Do not send mixed signals.

Realize the power of your words.

Appreciate it when people engage with you.

Socially intelligent people understand the function and the importance of effective and consistent communication. If you can make these things a habit, you will see its good effects. When you see the importance of it, you will be driven to put more time and effort into communication.

7

PAY ATTENTION TO OTHER PEOPLE

*I*t is true that people are wired differently. Some people are extroverts and others can be introverts by nature, too. Extroverts get a little more advantage when it comes to honing their communication skills because they tend to get more practice over introverts.

However, there is a way for anyone, introverted or not, to better their communication without having to express themselves too much and that is to practice active listening.

If social interactions are a two-way street, then aside from learning to express yourself you also have to learn to pay attention to other people. Although the goal of most people who are in pursuit of developing their social intelligence is to be heard and understood, there is power in learning from others too.

By listening to and observing others, you can help nurture your social intelligence. The mere act of paying attention to others without necessarily opening up is a very effective way to learn how to establish successful interpersonal relationships.

One struggle in being introverted is that they are drained whenever they engage in socialization. They do not dislike people. They just have a lower stock of energy intended for social interactions. They would rather reserve this energy for more meaningful connections.

For those who prefer to keep their social circles smaller, it is difficult to foster relationships and choose the persons you would want to connect with.

A benefit you can get from active listening is that as you try to understand other people more, you learn to trust and let them in. Being able to learn about them by mere observation and listening can help reserve your energy and make you better at choosing who you connect with.

If your social endurance is not an issue, active listening is still a very important skill to learn. The problem with those who find it easier to express themselves before trying to listen to the other person is that they lose sight of the real purpose of communication which is to connect.

I repeat: social interactions are a two-way street. If you go on and on without considering the effect you have on your audience, your words become useless and you do not gain anything from your encounter.

Stop telling yourself that you have done and said everything but you ended up with nothing. That is exactly the problem. It was just you that said and did everything. There was no exchange between you and the person you were trying to connect with. Ask yourself if you noticed any sort of response from that other person. If you got nothing, that counts as a response too.

If a dog keeps barking at you and no matter what you say or do he just continues to bark at you, would you stick around? Will you drain yourself out for something that does not entertain any response from you?

It is understandably difficult to restrain yourself when you are too excited or too frustrated about something. But it will only be a terrible waste of energy if you spill everything that matters to you and the person you shared it with just ends up too overwhelmed and unwilling to accommodate you further.

Focusing on paying attention to others is challenging. No one ever said it was easy but it is necessary if you want to improve on your social intelligence.

Here are some simple steps you can take to practice active listening:

1. DO NOT INTERRUPT.

This will require a lot of patience from you but it is worth the rewards.

Interrupting someone shows that you are not interested in whatever he or she has to say. You are flat out telling them, "No, my words are more important than yours".

Two things happen if you go down this road. One, you weaken your chances of having a meaningful exchange with this person. By not letting them have a voice in your conversation, you end up missing out on the things that are important to them. Without knowing what is valuable to them, you have nothing to offer to this person that is worth their while.

Two, you set a precedent of disrespect between

the two of you. The golden rule is still in effect when it comes to social intelligence. Do not do unto others what you do not want others to do unto you.

If you want to be respected, show the same courtesy to those you interact with.

If it is the other person that keeps interrupting you, just keep in mind that you are gaining more by not doing the same thing. Do not let him interfere with your process. Anything you practice constantly will become a habit and you must choose your habits wisely.

2. TAKE TIME TO THINK ABOUT WHAT SOMEONE ELSE IS SAYING BEFORE YOU RESPOND.

Do not listen just to respond. Keeping quiet is the farthest thing from active listening. If you are merely waiting for your turn to speak and you are not paying attention to what the other person is saying, you still end up failing at this task.

The main goal of active listening is to learn communication from others and tweak the social devices you make use of. When a person sees that their statements and opinions are valued, they are drawn to the listener more. Before you respond, see to it that you acknowledge what the other person has said. Really looking into what this person has said will also guide your response better.

For example, you want to eat pizza at an Italian restaurant. This person, on the other hand, keeps talking about seafood. Because you want to keep insisting on your favorite Italian restaurant, you forget that they actually serve seafood there, too. You had a good intention because you wanted to share something you enjoy with this person and you are convinced they will appreciate it as much as you do too. But instead of having a lovely time and getting both the things you want, you miss out on this opportunity because you were too focused and hasty with getting your ideas across.

3. TAKE CUES FROM PEOPLE AROUND YOU AND LEARN THE RIGHT BODY LANGUAGE.

Scan the room and take a look at how people are behaving around you and how everyone is participating in their own social interactions. You do not have to stare at them and scare them away. Just notice the simple things; a smile, a nod, a touch, their posture, their voice. See how their social exchanges work.

From there you will get an idea of how you can tweak your social devices. You also get an idea of what turns people off.

This may not seem like much but once you get into a similar situation as to what you have observed, you suddenly practice the things you have learned from this.

You may not notice it at first but if you routinely review the way you approach social situations, you might be able to recognize that you have applied what you learned from mere observation.

4. LISTEN TO THE INFLECTIONS IN WHAT OTHERS SAY, WHICH CAN GIVE YOU CLUES TO WHAT THE PERSON REALLY MEANS.

Inflections keep languages dynamic and make it fully customizable to any person when needed. There is a cliché that women are not really okay when they simply say "OK".

This is because people are making use of a trick inflections do to words. In fact, inflections have evolved with the wider use of text language. "K." and "okay <3" now have different meanings even though the base words are the same. This shows just how important it is to take note of inflections. A lot of misunderstandings occur when the changes in inflections are not acknowledged. This is an instance where paying attention to people becomes really handy.

To keep your focus in paying attention to people, find the value in your interaction. Think clearly about why you are interacting with this person.

Do you work with this person? If yes, then think about how your interactions with them affect the camaraderie and productivity in the office.

Do you enjoy this person? If yes, then remind yourself that getting to know someone requires paying attention to the things they like, things that motivate them, and things that disappoint them.

Paying attention to people is a social currency as well. You only get what you give. So invest time and energy in giving attention to other people too. Not only will it enable you to build stronger connections, but it will also foster a more positive and respectful culture within your relationships.

8

LOOKING AT THINGS FROM
SOMEONE ELSE'S PERSPECTIVE

*C*ontinuing with the importance of paying attention to other people, one of the things we all have to learn about others is that everyone has different experiences that affect the things they do today.

Maybe the world would have been a more peaceful place if everyone shared similar perspectives. However, it would have made this world quite boring and we humans would not have made much progress if that was the case.

There are those who were raised in individualistic societies and there are those who were raised in societies that encourage a sense of belongingness within a tribe or within a family. Some people were also taught to prioritize standing out in a crowd.

These differences define our lives but these differences also mean we will always be in opposition to others. It does not matter who they are and what the circumstances are. You will have differences with your spouse, your boss, your family, and even your friends.

It is not a question of who is right and who is wrong. What makes things difficult is when people assume that their beliefs are better and more correct than those of others. This creates resentment and animosity leading to damaged relationships and failed communication. You will see this happen in autocratic societies where subordinates are given low motivation and have developed resentment towards their leaders.

Respecting the views and perspectives of others is necessary for fostering successful interpersonal relationships. When their values and ideas are respected, people are more willing to participate fairly and happily in social interactions. You only get what you give.

Imagine having a conversation with someone about the food that you enjoy. If you enjoy rice and that person doesn't, it will be terrible if he tells you that rice is impossible to like and that you should stop liking it. How will this make you feel?

This other person has no regard for how this thing matters to you because he thinks what he knows and what he prefers is the standard. If you are dealing with such a person, are you still willing to continue engaging in a conversation with them?

What more if the rice had so much value in your life? What if it is the only thing you have in life as a source of food and nutrition? It will surely make you feel like this person has no ability whatsoever of being able to see what is valuable to another person. Your needs do not matter much to him. If that was the case, then why would you bother opening yourself up to them when they seem like they do not have the capacity to accommodate what is essential to others?

That person could be you if you do not make an effort to see things in someone else's eyes and if you do not see value in other people's circumstances, feelings, and beliefs.

This, however, does not automatically mean that you have to adopt the views that are opposite to yours. You reverse the situation, then, and you end up with your own resentments and failed communication.

What looking at other people's perspective requires you to do is to keep an open mind and make it your goal to fully understand what others have to say. If you have the right to be heard and hold a different opinion that is your own, then others should also have the same rights as you.

Listening fully to the ideals and principles of others leads you to the right actions and forms of communication you need to apply to be able to build a strong relationship with others. This is not because your ideas do not matter, this is because you are dealing with another person who has his own feelings and own convictions. The only way you can live and work together is by respecting each other's priorities and boundaries.

If you are wrong, then change. If you are right, then hold your ground. Respect is not equal to submission. Respect is the acceptance and acknowledgment of the things that are essential to each person's happiness and fulfillment.

You can maintain a level of respect even when you do not agree with another person's views. Explain why your ideals are important without making the person feel like they do not matter. Strive to state your feelings, opinions, and beliefs tactfully and with clarity. If you are dealing with a sensible person, you will be understood and heard.

If not, then it is best to avoid conflict and exit

yourself from this gracefully. There is no need for you to lose your kindness if you are unable to convince others of your ideals. This just means that there is no possible way for you and this other person to accommodate each of your own set of standards in this circumstance.

A study done in Iowa showed that there are people who are not able to adjust their beliefs even if they are faced with valid pieces of evidence that oppose their sentiments. This circles back to how that person is wired and the other values that he prioritizes because of the environment he was raised in.

Comprehending someone else's point of view does not stop with understanding the statements they give. Place yourself in the shoes of others and try to also understand what they feel versus just what they think. Every person has his own way of processing the things he sees and every person's experiences will always be different from yours.

When we speak, we all have our own biases, values, and beliefs that affect the way we conclude and respond. Seeing the world through eyes other than our own will enable us to understand what is important to others, what moves them, and what is non-negotiable to them.

This will take a lot of humility and patience for you to practice. However, the very reason why people are able to improve their lives through social intelligence is that they recognize that they are not the only people who matter in this world. Everywhere you go, you have to work with people who have their own set of emotions, principles, and values.

Once you see things from their perspective, you can start communicating in ways that appeal to their unique manner of expression and accommodate what is essential to their being. Doing so will make people trust and open up to you more. It breaks down their barriers and it enables them to cooperate with you more because they feel valued and understood.

When you are faced with a person you cannot seem to understand. You must acknowledge that as well. You do not go on and intrude on another person's life and impose things on them especially when you do not have a good understanding of that person's life.

It is never okay to assume that because a person does not speak his mind he completely agrees with everything you say and do. You can only have an idea of what others value and prefer but your understanding will never be enough for you to decide for them.

When a person is so closed off, there is no way for you to completely tell if you are on the same page with him or her. This can be quite difficult, of course. But we again have to go back to how this person is raised and how this person is wired.

You do not necessarily have to dig up a person's past or put them in a box made up of your own limited set of standards and views of the world. All you can do is treat this situation with even more respect and understanding.

For some people, it takes a lot more time and trust for them to open up to other people. And there are also people who are not able to open up completely. These people may place a lot of value on their privacy. They may have had traumatizing experiences in the past. Or maybe they just do not see it as a priority to reveal themselves to you.

That is why you also do not go barging into their lives and require them to open up to you when they are not willing and ready. There are advantages for every person if they are able to communicate what matters to them but this is not something that should be forced. In no way is opening up to you the responsibility of any person. If you want to get to know someone, you have to be patient and you have to allow them to go about this at their own pace.

It is never productive to blame someone for not freely letting you into their lives. This is also a sign that you do not see things from the other person's perspective. You are only taking care of your own needs and requirements.

What you can do is to make a safe zone for them to comfortably and willingly share their inner thoughts and beliefs with you. The more this happens, the more opportunities you get at understanding the other person better.

If this never happens with them, respect that. That person will appreciate it more if you are able to leave them with their preferred devices. This shows that you do not prioritize your needs before others and that you are able to recognize their values too. Who knows, this may even show them that you are worthy of their trust and confidence and they later proceed to share more of themselves with you.

If the person ends up suffering because of their inability to communicate, remember that this is not your lesson to learn. A good person wishes good things for others. If it does not work out for him, practice kindness. If it works out for him, wish him more happiness and success. But never make his actions your responsibility.

Looking at everything from another person's perspective is a humble acknowledgment that you do not know everything and that you do not have the monopoly to automatically know what is right for everyone. Socially intelligent people recognize that in order to participate well in a social setting, you have to realize that no two people can ever be the same. Work on getting to know people and looking at life from different perspectives.

9

RESPECT CULTURAL DIFFERENCES

*A*s we have gathered from our previous chapter, we all have our own set of experiences that made us into who we are today. That is the very reason why we all have differences that sometimes clash with each other. Most people learn and acquire skills through their friends, family, and the community around them. Understanding that the way people respond and the customs they practice are greatly affected by their upbringing.

The foundation of our beliefs, values, rituals, and skills was formed based on the culture of the societies we were raised in. Our culture is what guides us in the social system of the community we were born into.

Each culture has its own set of regulations and

forms of justice based on their history and needs. This dictates the actions, rituals, and standards we follow to be able to keep harmony within the societies we are living in. Culture also provides us with a framework to follow so that we can better understand others and work well with those who belong to the same community.

When we are placed in a situation where the context of the culture is unfamiliar to us, we feel unequipped and we are unable to navigate as easily as we do with those who share the same cultural practices with us.

This may be the initial reaction you have when put in such a position but a better way of looking at it is to see it as an opportunity to gain valuable knowledge about the world, other cultures, and how your very own culture is perceived by others.

All cultures have their own language, traditions, beliefs, clothing, and laws that organize their society. These things are unique to each culture and are indicative of their accomplishments and history. Some cultures even took thousands of years to be established. The very reason why these cultures were able to survive thousands of years and are passed on from generation to generation is that society recognizes it exists and accepts it because it is seen essential to keep their societies thriving.

How do you invalidate something that has provided fulfillment and harmony to the lives of many for so long? Well, that is something that the whole world continues to struggle with. And the main reason behind it is that people find it hard to understand that managing interpersonal relations does not require you to invalidate the culture of others. In fact, it is better to accept that each person's culture is valuable and legitimate in his society, his life, and the world we live in.

What we have to do is to overcome the fears we have when we are faced with a culture that is different from ours. We can only do this by first recognizing that there are many cultures that have emerged and thrived around the world.

You yourself have your own culture that you follow. It does not have to be a culture that was formed thousands of years ago. Look at the social devices you use and the rituals, traditions, and habits you follow within your family and the community you grew up in. Every person has a values system that is based on how he was raised and the environment he lives in. This can be considered a form of culture as well.

No culture is more valid than others. Saying that one culture is less valid devalues the people who are living in the society in which that culture comes from. And just the same, no person should also be forced to erase their culture to accommodate another's. This applies to you and anybody else in the world.

Taking his culture away from a person is an injustice that destroys a person's self-worth and self-image. You are taking his sense of identity away from him and showing him that everything he has learned up to this point is of no value and therefore he must adopt a different sense of identity. No one but the person himself has the right to decide what will bring peace and joy in his life.

Once you gain the understanding and the confidence towards facing your own culture and the culture of others, you can begin to open yourself up to the opportunity of learning and accepting other people's cultures.

Having an unconditional and unprejudiced mindset is the first requirement for understanding a culture that is not your own. Exploring and learning about culture will require your full openness, appreciation, and respect for others. You have to recognize that you are dealing with matters that are valuable to a person and the society he belongs to. Societies and the people that belong to them are rooted in their culture and you are rooted in your very own culture too.

Learning about the values, traditions, and beliefs of others is also a way for you to have a deeper understanding of your own culture. By looking at how others manage their lives based on their culture, you are able to parallel and contrast your way of life to that of others. You realize what social traditions, priorities, and rituals you have based on the similarities and differences you find with the other person.

As you get a better understanding of how cultures are formed and what it does for people, you find more reason and purpose in your life and the lives of others too. You realize the meaning and thinking behind the values systems that exist within societies.

With acceptance and understanding, it becomes easier for you to respect diversity. This is very difficult to achieve if you only see things from your perspective.

It also becomes easier to keep an open mind to the intricacies of other cultures once you realize that cultural diversity leads to growth and prosperity.

Tea is a part of Asian culture that was able to

thrive and be accepted in European culture as well. Many of the things we enjoy today like chocolates, spices, arts, and design resulted from the effects of cultural exchange and globalization.

When new ideas are accepted without prejudice it can make way for new solutions and opportunities. It also paves the way for new alternatives and sources of knowledge. There is so much to benefit from learning and giving value to diversity and the first step to it is allowing yourself to open your mind to it.

There are several ways for you to familiarize your mind and immerse yourself in learning about the culture of others.

One, participate, and actively listen to conversations with people who have a different culture from yours. Enter the conversations with an open heart and an open mind. Try to find the rationale and the appreciation for the differences you find with them.

Do not actively search for things to disagree with. If something does not sound right to you, try and put yourself in the other person's shoes and see why it matters to them. Do not judge them based on your orientation.

The very reason for your differences with them is the compilation of traditions, values, and experiences they have within the society they came from.

Be respectful and understand that although you disagree with them, it is important to them and their culture. Always offer kindness and understanding first.

Two, learn more about the culture of others by collecting information from various sources. Watch the movies they make, listen to their music, and read up about their culture and history. Their history and the stories they tell are good sources of information on how and why their values system was formed.

You can make learning an enjoyable experience. Keep it exciting so that your interest grows as you immerse yourself in this cultural experience. This is also something that you can easily share with others and it can lead to meaningful conversations about cultural diversity that everyone can learn something from.

It is easier more than ever to have access to more material about cultural diversity because of the internet. With the rise of social media, people around the world are able to connect at a faster pace and with more accessibility.

Always remember to practice being sensitive as well. If something is very important to someone's beliefs, do not make fun of it. Some cultures have their own religious practices and it is important to be aware of these things. If you do not understand it, do not make fun of it and speak too freely about it. If you want to have an understanding of their customs and traditions, respectfully ask the right questions and do proper research about it.

If you have gathered information about their beliefs and practices, be sensitive about how you share your learnings with others. This is also a form of respect that you should give to other people. Sharing wrong and misleading information about their culture is unfair and it can lead to more tensions rather than understanding.

Three, travel as much as you can. Studies have shown that people who travel a lot and people who migrate to other countries far from their own tend to be more tolerant and have better-developed communication skills than those that stay close to home.

Traveling and moving to another country forces you to orient yourself more with the culture of others. Being a foreigner also requires you to learn the language, respect customs that are different from yours, follow a system that is new to you, base your actions on their existing framework and social etiquette. All of which will be very beneficial to your social intelligence.

As you get more comfortable in places other than

your hometown, you also realize that there is nothing to be scared about when it comes to diversity. You place more meaning and value on your own culture too. Instead of losing your identity, you even strengthen it.

Making the move to explore cultural diversity requires patience, kindness, understanding, and a whole lot of heart and effort. It may seem like a daunting task at first but you just have to remind yourself that you have nothing to lose and a lot to gain in this process.

Your social intelligence grows as you accept and understand the fact that everyone is built in a different way. It is counterproductive to ask others to adjust according to your orientation and standards.

The sooner you realize this, the more time you have for yourself to learn and do better socially. With more time on your hands, the more opportunities for socialization you get and the more chances you have at tweaking the bad habits you want to get rid of. It also allows you to pace yourself better and not get overwhelmed with the many things you can learn from. Remind yourself to appreciate the journey and avoid unnecessary pressures that can lead you to resent this exercise.

10

LEARN HOW TO RESOLVE CONFLICTS

*C*onflict is inevitable in any social setting. As previously discussed, people have varying views, opinions, and feelings about certain things. These differences are bound to create conflicts and misunderstandings.

Social disputes can make or break relationships. But if a conflict is handled respectfully and positively, it can be a way to strengthen bonds and build trust within relationships. You should hone your conflict resolution skills to further improve your social intelligence.

To do this, you must first have a better understanding of how conflicts work.

Some people say they would rather avoid conflicts but what does that do? You can never find someone who thinks and feels exactly the way you do one hundred percent of the time. Conflicts will arise one way or another and when conflicts are not confronted, it does not resolve itself. The emotions you feel might temporarily fade away but since the issue has never been resolved, it comes back up. It only takes another trigger and you are back to those feelings again.

Our differences do not automatically create conflicts. Differences become a problem when a person thinks and feels that his values, desires, motivations, and ideas are compromised in the relationship. Every person has his own set of deep, personal needs that is exclusive to him. The issues may appear trivial to someone else and that is where the problem lies.

Here is an example of conflicting needs:

Toddlers have a yearning to learn and explore. Their curiosity can sometimes lead to unsafe situations like climbing up windows or wandering off somewhere without their parents. However, parents are motivated to protect their kids and they can only do this by setting rules and limitations. These are opposing needs and it eventually leads to conflicts.

When conflicts arise, a person's need to feel safe, valued, and respected and his need for closeness and intimacy are perceived to be threatened. If such concerns are not addressed, it can result in arguments, distance, and breakups in personal relationships. In a working environment, this can result in a decrease in productivity, bad transactions, and lost opportunities.

Successful long-term relationships have to consider the needs of each person. If all parties decide to assess their conflicting needs with respect and compassion, this can pave the way for stronger team relations and creative resolutions.

Because people tend to perceive disagreements as a threat, it needs to be addressed properly so that it does not lead to strong negative emotions. Our life experiences, culture, and values system affect our perceptions of things and the way we react to them.

Managing the emotions that come with these perceptions in times of stress will be difficult if the person has not mastered it yet. It can be impossible to come up with a successful resolution if this was the situation.

For people to address these worries more easily, they should see conflicts as an opportunity for growth more than a battleground. The fear of conflict can skew your perspective of things and take your focus away from problem solving and resolution. Removing this fear is more challenging for people who have been in traumatizing unhealthy relationships and painful experiences from previous disagreements. These people tend to view conflict as a terrifying, demoralizing, or humiliating situation.

Feeling threatened whenever you confront conflicts can be a problem. You will likely respond to conflict by closing off or expressing things with bias and sometimes anger. This is not a healthy way of managing and addressing disagreements. When conflict is confronted in an unhealthy manner, this will lead to disappointment and uncertainty. It can cause resentments, irreparable relationships, and distance.

A healthier approach to a conflict requires respect and understanding.

Choosing to be respectful in conflict resolution will guide a person's words and actions during a confrontation. When you respect the other person, you make the effort to be calm and non-adversarial in your speech and conduct.

Calmness plays an important role in communicating and keeping your conversation organized. Keeping calm during conflict resolution requires patience. It is easy to lose your calm when you become too eager to convey your side of things and while the other person is laying down his thoughts. If you truly respect your peer, you will be patient in this process and not prioritize your own feelings and thoughts because you place value in the other person too.

Being non-adversarial means you participate appropriately in the process, you pay attention to the other person, you practice active listening, and you avoid being defensive. When you respect someone's time, effort, and needs, you make it a point to listen to them properly.

If you do not intend to listen to the other person, the respectful thing to do is to be clear about it and not deceive them into thinking that you are here to have an exchange of thoughts. Do not just pretend to listen.

Unfortunately, if you do not consider the other person's side, there is a good chance that your resolution is incomplete and another conflict will arise eventually.

Now let's talk about being understanding. Understanding someone requires compassion and attention. Compassion is sometimes mistaken for being patronizing and condescending. Being compassionate does not mean you view the other person as someone beneath you. It does not mean that the other person is pitiful or incapable.

Showing compassion means you can recognize the difficulties of the person. When you are compassionate, you accompany that person throughout his difficulties by responding based on the emotions and thoughts that are brought about by his situation.

In conflict resolution, this means that you recognize that this person's needs are also on the line and his participation is based on an effort to try and balance his needs with yours. This allows you to set aside your biases and become more attentive to his needs as well. Being compassionate does not mean you give more priority to the other person's concerns. It only means you consider why this is a challenge for the other person too.

When you are committed to tackling conflicts in a healthy manner, the foundation of your resolution is strong and you can navigate through it more successfully.

It is now time for you to take note of your abilities. The success of your resolution will depend on your abilities.

The ability to manage stress – Stress can affect your perceptions and your communication. Resolving conflicts can be stressful because you are considering not just your issues but also your peers. If you can keep yourself calm and composed under pressure, your communication is clearer and you get to listen and understand the other person more accurately.

The ability to control your emotions – You have to understand your own needs to be able to communicate them with clarity.

If you are aware of your emotions, it is easier for you to pinpoint what exactly it is that is bothering you. You do not go haywire and spew unnecessary and irrelevant issues. Recognize your emotional state and what causes these strong feelings.

This will allow you to control your emotions and focus on what really matters. Do not let your emotions control you. You should be able to communicate your issues without resorting to threats, intimidation, and retaliation.

The ability to listen – Here is where you should be able to practice active listening. It becomes more difficult to practice active listening if you are stressed and if you have a lot of strong feelings about the situation. However, your understanding of the whole picture relies heavily on how you interpret and understand the other person's side.

The ability to assess differences fairly – Your

differences with your peers goes both ways. Remind yourself to see things fairly and to respect the other party's needs. The amount of respect you expect should be equal to the amount of respect you give.

Take note of what level of these abilities you have by looking at your previous experiences with conflict resolution. Assess where you are lacking and what the causes are. The next time you have the need to resolve conflicts again, remind yourself of these abilities and observe whether there are things you find more difficult than others.

SOME TIPS ON CONFLICT RESOLUTION:

The first thing to remember about resolving conflicts is that the goal is not to win or be right. The goal is to strengthen and maintain relationships. You are arguing not to argue, you are arguing to settle both you and your peer's issues.

Pace yourself. Resolving conflict takes up time and energy. Prioritize and focus on the present. Sometimes you have multiple issues you want to resolve. When this happens, organize your thoughts and manage your emotions first. Ask yourself if all of them really matter today.

Do not let previous conflicts get entangled

with the present. You will only find it more difficult to communicate clearly and assess both you
and your peer's issues accurately if you keep
bringing up issues that happened in the past.
Holding grudges and placing blames will only
clutter your mind and put a strain on your
emotions.

Pick your battles. Some conflicts are not worth
your time and energy to resolve. If you see a
stranger's comment on the internet that is against
your beliefs, think about how much it matters to you
first and if it is worth your time and energy to discuss
things with this stranger.

Agree to disagree. Sometimes you just cannot
come to an agreement. Recognize when things are
going nowhere. Let go and move on. You have to
know when to stop and. You do not have to have the
last word. Do not let pointless arguments drain you.
All it does is make you angry and resentful.

Conflict resolution should be looked at as a case
to case basis. No disagreement can be tackled the
same way. There is no formula for it. You have to
approach it with patience and diligence.

Although there is no formula for conflict resolution, you can equip yourself with the abilities and the
framework we discussed in this chapter. Treat your

disagreements with understanding and respect the outcome of your resolution.

If you truly aim to harness your social intelligence, then approach conflict resolutions respectfully and objectively.

11

WORK ON INCREASING YOUR
EMOTIONAL INTELLIGENCE

*E*motional intelligence (EI) is about the ability of a person to recognize, evaluate, and take control of his emotions. It is similar to social intelligence in that it requires you to evaluate and interpret concepts founded on yourself and others. However, emotional intelligence is more focused on being able to empathize and assess things based on emotions.

Studies have led researchers to assign four different levels of EI. These levels are emotional perception, the ability to reason using emotions, the ability to understand emotion, and the ability to manage emotions.

These four aspects of emotional intelligence are arranged by complexities relating to the processes that go hand in hand with them. The more basic levels involve perceiving and expressing emotions and the higher levels require more conscious involvement and regulation.

Emotional perception means you must have the ability to accurately perceive emotions. This involves being able to read into nonverbal language and facial expressions. Through emotional perception, you recognize your feelings and you identify them. You know the differences between being happy, sad, and angry and you attach those labels to certain how they feel.

Next, the ability to reason using emotions means a person is able to use feelings to stimulate thoughts and cognitive activity. The focus of his reactions and what he pays attention can be motivated by emotions. The reason why robots are not considered emotionally intelligent is that all their actions and responses are based on command and logic. Robots will not be able to adjust their responses depending on emotions because they simply do not have feelings.

Third, the ability to understand emotions enables people to assign meanings to emotions. If a person is showing expressions of sadness, the interpretation is that the person is sad and that there are reasons for his sadness.

For example, you find your spouse crying quietly in the bedroom, this will lead you to think something must have happened that made her upset. It may be because you have said or done something that was offensive to your partner. Maybe your spouse is having some problems at work or with your kids.

Lastly, the highest level of emotional intelligence is being able to manage emotions effectively. It is vital to have the capability to regulate emotions and respond to other people's emotions appropriately. You need to be able to separate your thoughts and feelings.

You do not think you are angry. You feel you are angry. You do not feel that laptops are better than desktop computers. You think that laptops are better than desktop computers.

In emotional intelligence, to be able to feel connotes emotions and to be able to think entails rational thoughts. You have to identify between the two so that you know whether you have to manage your emotions or adjust your thoughts before deciding on an action.

Emotional Intelligence greatly impacts social intelligence because the capabilities associated with it will greatly influence the way you participate in a social setting. Imagine not being able to tell how your friend feels when you are having a conversation with him. If your friend keeps a straight face and a monotone voice the whole time you are with him. That is exactly what it is like when you are not able to identify emotions and emotional responses.

These are some ways emotional intelligence influences social intelligence:

GREATER SELF-AWARENESS

A key factor in having self-awareness is being able to consider the things that affect emotions. This allows you to understand and manage your own feelings better.

When you are talking to your boss about the workload and the schedule of your deadlines, you start to notice that your boss is becoming antagonized as you speak. You look back on this encounter and you start to realize that you were behaving according to emotions of frustration and fear. As you were explaining to him your situation, you apparently started raising your voice and your face started to show anger. Your words started to sound like you were putting blame on him.

These actions were triggered by strong emotions. If you are not aware of how you speak and how you behave based on the emotions you are having, it can lead to misunderstandings and mishandled conflict resolutions.

THINKING BEFORE REACTING

Recognizing that emotions are temporary enables emotionally intelligent people to not be overpowered by them. Taking time to regulate your emotions before reacting to a highly emotional situation will enable you to calm down and tackle things rationally and more accurately.

When you are experiencing strong feelings of anger, you resort to actions that are meant to attack or to retaliate. You start placing blame, threatening people, and looking for ways to punish their perceived offenses towards you.

Also, anger tends to take over your perception of things and your ability to express sentiments. When you are angry, you tend to focus on feelings of being attacked and whatever the other person says may sound offensive and inadequate to you.

When you have a strong motivation to express

your anger, it also becomes a challenge to be clear about your statements.

For example, you are angry because your significant other forgot about your birthday and a deal you were working hard to close did not push through. This will be a combination of two stressful things that can push you to feel anger.

You start shouting at your significant other and you spew words you do not mean. This transpires and it causes even more stressful consequences.

What you could have done was separate your feelings between the two situations. Once you start managing these feelings, think clearly about what you really want. Anger is temporary and it is an emotion that can come from frustration.

Maybe you just want your significant other to say sorry to you. Maybe you wanted to spend time with that person but it did not happen. Managing your feelings can allow you to express these needs more clearly and when you are clear about your intentions, the other person finds it easier to address your needs.

EMPATHIZING WITH OTHERS

Empathizing with how others are feeling is a huge part of emotional intelligence. People who are emotionally intelligent consider the perspectives, emotions, and experiences of others as the basis for other people's actions. This is why it helps to see yourself in the shoes of others to be able to empathize with them.

Looking at things rationally is not always enough especially in a social setting. Being able to consider both reason and emotion is more effective in building strong interpersonal relationships. People operate on different levels and the more aware you are of this, the easier for you to identify the best approach.

This is a common problem in the workplace. People try to be as professional as possible when they are in the office. Their focus is on productivity and efficiency.

Sometimes, people get overwhelmed by the pressures of transactions. People get frustrated, angry, and unappreciated but because they concentrate too much at work, they do not recognize how this has already triggered strong emotions in them.

This creates conflicts that can only be resolved if you tackle it from an emotional standpoint. If a person has feelings of being unfulfilled and underappreciated, maybe all that person needs is a pat on the back.

There are also conflicts that seem like they can

be tackled rationally but actually entails an emotional approach as well. For example, someone forgets about emailing a client. That person resolved it and the client was satisfied with the actions taken.

From a rational point of view, the work was done effectively and the client did not mind the mistake. But, the other coworkers involved still feel bad about the issue. What is missing?

First, the person needs to apologize for his mistake. Second, he needs to alleviate the frustrations of his coworkers, as well. To do both, he needs to have an understanding of how emotions work.

Although it appears to be an inborn characteristic, researchers propose that it is possible to learn and hone emotional intelligence.

Harnessing your emotional intelligence also enables you to take criticism objectively, be accountable for your actions, communicate your feelings more clearly, respond, and pay attention to others better. It also allows you to consider all parties during problem-solving and make clear and accurate decisions for yourself.

There are steps you can take to hone your emotional intelligence.

1. EMPATHIZE

Understand someone else's point of view by putting yourself in their shoes. Think about how you would feel when placed in the person's situation. When you empathize with others, you understand things from an emotional standpoint. You recognize the nuances of their speech and actions and you are able to assign what types of emotions are influencing their reactions.

Emotions have their patterns as well and once you get to see these patterns, it becomes easier for you to recognize what is happening to a person emotionally.

Some people tend to bite their nails when they are worried. There are people who start talking too much when they are nervous. There are people whose first reaction raise their voices when they are frustrated. These patterns depend from person to person but can be common to others as well. When you are so used to reading through these signals, empathy becomes instinctive to you and the more you practice empathy, the stronger your emotional intelligence will be.

2. LISTEN

Pay attention to others and listen sincerely. Take note of their nonverbal cues as well. Body language is difficult to feign so being able to interpret nonverbal language can be helpful in understanding others.

Listening is a very important tool in empathy as well. When you are able to accommodate the viewpoints of another person, you realize how you can empathize with him more easily. You consider different factors that are contributing to that person's emotions.

When he says he is lonely, you can better empathize with this sentiment of his. You start to understand why he keeps trying to look for a company all the time. You realize why he has not been having enough sleep recently. You receive explanations for the emotions and actions you want to understand.

3. INTROSPECT

Take a look at how your behavior and reactions are influenced by your emotions. Consider also how the emotions of others affect their responses when placed in the same situation as yours. This requires the ability to reason with your emotions. Understand what roles emotions play in your decision making and behavior as well as others'.

Here are some more questions to guide through introspection:

What effects do your emotions have on your interpretation of events and social interactions?

Are your emotions stable and consistent? How fast do you move on from one emotion to another? Take note of the levels of the emotions you have as well.

Are you able to identify the triggers of your emotions? Do you experience strong emotions when you are by yourself?

Do your emotions manifest physiologically? For example, do you experience stomach aches when you are worried or sad? You can use these as cues to be able to identify your feelings more accurately.

Does your body language match your emotions?

Do your feelings lead to strong expressions that affect you and others? How does it impact others? When you are mad, do you have a tendency to project these feelings on others?

Allowing some time for yourself to assess your emotions can be a learning experience that will greatly affect your perception of life and your ability to foster more meaningful relationships.

If you are having a hard time getting to know yourself in terms of your emotions, try reaching out to friends and family. Read more about it and make a conscious effort to assess yourself.

Having strong emotional intelligence will also enable you to choose interactions wisely. When a person makes you angry or frustrated, find your triggers. If the triggers come from that person's behavior and you find no way to resolve this with him, then he may not be worth your time and energy.

There is such a thing as an emotionally draining relationship. Usually, this involves a person who is considered an emotional vampire. Have you ever had an interaction with someone and you just felt utterly drained after? That person could be an emotional vampire.

Dr. Judith Orloff, MD is an assistant clinical professor of psychiatry at UCLA who wrote about emotional vampires in her book, *Emotional Freedom: Liberate Yourself from Negative Emotions and Transform Your Life.* An emotional vampire feeds off the emotional energy of other people and there are several types of it.

THE NARCISSIST

These people place too much self-importance in themselves. They hog attention and are motivated by large doses of admiration. They can be eloquent and intelligent that is why they draw people in.

Indulging someone for their good qualities is not a terrible thing to do. What you have to do is find a way to provide his need for validation as you try to let yourself into the conversation too. If your methods do not work, then exit yourself gracefully.

THE VICTIM

There are people who always find ways to make themselves look like the victim and think that the world is always against him. They drown in self-pity and they demand to be rescued or excused.

You must recognize that you do not have to be a part of his narrative if it does not really involve you. Do not fool yourself into thinking you can save him. At the end of the day, it is impossible to save someone who is comfortable with being troubled.

THE CONTROLLER

They tend to be self-righteous and they seem to have an opinion about everything. They try to place judgments and make it seem like they are the authority on what is right and wrong.

When you encounter people like this, assert your needs but know when to stop. It is hard to be effective with people like this. They cannot be managed so you have to agree to disagree and come up with methods that will allow you to avoid interacting with them.

THE CRITICIZER

Similar to the controller, they see themselves as the authority. However, a criticizer will make you feel ashamed and unqualified. They do this to lift their ego.

Do not take what he says personally and speak up only when needed. Taking things personally will only make you defensive and it will only create a loop. This person has a hunger for validation. Appreciate their useful insight but recognize when you have had enough.

THE SPLITTER

He is driven by strong emotions. One day he is so good to you and then becomes ruthless to you once he feels offended even at the slightest. He is like a ticking time bomb dressed in gems.

You have to set your boundaries when you are dealing with such a person. Be objective in your actions and do not get sucked into his vortex. Be aware of who you are and refuse to take sides.

It will be easier for you to identify emotional vampires once you polish on your emotional intelligence. Be self-aware and be careful not to become an emotional vampire as well. People will most likely find a way to avoid you if they start to notice that interactions with you are draining them for no good reason too.

Being socially and emotionally intelligent does not mean you have to be okay with everybody. There are people who will strain you emotionally and you have to be aware of this. This will affect the way you perform at work, the way you manage your social energy, and the way you look at relationships.

Emotional and social intelligence can simply give you the tools to understand and manage your social interactions better. You are not required to feed anyone else's ego if it already consumes too much of you. Empathy does not mean you have to rescue people. Empathizing with people only means you are able to see the other person's reasoning as influenced by his emotions.

Be careful with your social endurance. People who have a higher EI tend to get consumed because they easily tap into other people's emotions. Remember that you are still your own person and your issues are separate from others. Do not involve yourself in the problems of others but make adjustments to the way you conduct your interactions with them as guided by that person's emotional status.

12

APPRECIATE THE IMPORTANT PEOPLE IN YOUR LIFE

*A*cquiring social intelligence involves interacting with different people. You make an effort to try and foster relationships but you cannot expect to have the same level of relationship with everyone you interact with. It is important that you are able to invest in deep relationships with people who you find are meaningful to you.

But, how do you find meaning in relationships?

It is easy to look at our interactions with people as mere transactions. You meet a waiter, you order from him, he serves you, you finish your meal, and then you are out the door. The interaction is rooted entirely on the fact that you wanted to eat and the waiter was doing his job. He needed the sale from you and you needed the product from him.

But what if we change a few things in this interaction?

You take your seat, and then he hands you the menu.

You look at his nametag and you tell him, "Good morning, Jeff. How are you today?" as you go through the menu options.

The waiter replies, "Oh, my morning has been great so far, how about you?"

You proceed to have a very brief chat with him and then he hands you your order.

After eating, you tell him you had a great meal, you thank him, and tell him to have a good day.

You do this at least every other day with this person. After a few weeks, you have started feeling a connection with this person. He is not solely the waiter at the cafe anymore. He is now Jeff. He lives a few blocks away from the cafe. He is a part-timer who studies at the nearby college. Once Jeff eventually leaves his job, it will somehow be a significant change in your life and you will have to rewire yourself when someone replaces him.

Jeff now holds some value in your life. It is because you have acknowledged his presence, he was listened to, he was seen, he had a name. And he did the same for you. This is a person that now plays a role in your life. Even if it is a small role, he has still established a more meaningful relationship with you.

It is easy to get so preoccupied with our lives that we end up not acknowledging the people we interact with. We forget to make people matter. The first requirement in social intelligence is that you see people for who they are. This includes their identity, their feelings, and their actions. When we only look at their function in our everyday transactions, it is impossible to have a meaningful relationship with them.

When there is no meaning in the things we do, we are not fulfilled and we end up unhappy. One way to find meaning in life is to feel that you genuinely belong. Psychologists say this is because it satisfies two conditions in someone's life. One is being in a relationship that is based on mutual care. Because of this, you feel you are validated. You are treated like you matter so you feel that you really do matter.

Two, because you are able to enjoy moments of joy and fun consistently with a person. The interaction between the customer and Jeff has brought a sense of belongingness to the both of them because they participate in enjoyable interactions often. This is a way to endear someone to you. That is why when you see a cute toddler, you want both of you to enjoy the presence of each other. You make an effort to endear yourself to the toddler. You make jokes, you act silly, and you find a way to make it fun.

A sense of belongingness is not automatic in relationships. This requires constant effort from both parties. This comes in many forms.

For example, when you are on a long road trip with your friend, the person sitting in the passenger's seat tries his best not to fall asleep. This is an effort he is making because he does not want you to feel alone in the task of driving.

Another example is when you are watching a movie with your significant other, you offer a gesture to acknowledge your significant other. You can initiate holding hands or you try to lean against your partner more. When your partner responds according to the signals you send, you feel validated and the bond grows. You have made a way to share a moment with this person and it was accepted.

If these small gestures are able to fulfill a person's sense of belongingness, it is easy to make a person feel unwanted too.

How does this work? Say you ask the lady at the front desk of your office if they received a package for you. As she hands you the package, she tells you that your kids go to the same daycare. You just looked at her and ignored her remark. You were focused solely on the transaction and you just did not take notice of her effort. This lady is then left feeling rejected. You were not able to make any connection with her because you just saw her as a variable in a transaction.

You would think this only affects the lady. However, psychologists have found that when someone is rejected, the rejecter also alienates himself and will feel insignificant after the encounter. Whenever you pass by the front desk, a part of you may feel this alienation too and you would feel the need to avoid her. This is because the bond that the lady wanted to offer to you has been dismissed.

But it does not have to end there. If you really make an effort to fix things between the two of you, it is possible to have an opportunity for trust-building again. But this time, the offer of trust will have to come from you.

What you can do for the lady is to start an inter-action with her once more. This time, you offer kind-ness. You start greeting her with a smile whenever you arrive at the office. You call her by her name and thank her when you enlist her help. But do not forget to confirm that, yes, your kids go to the same daycare. It does not have to be a grand gesture but it has to be consistent and sincere.

It is not guaranteed that we can have the same exchanges in all the interactions we participate in. But being aware of how this works enables us to choose to reciprocate and understand others when we feel rejected. Since there is a consciousness about how we make others feel and how we all benefit from the process, it is now easier for you to take the necessary steps in building more meaningful relationships.

To further guide you in the journey of choosing the people you value in your life, here are a few things you can base your views on to help you appreciate people more.

1. EVERYONE IS DOING THE BEST THEY CAN

People will always try to do things with the best intentions. No person wants to mess things up in their life. Whether it be their lifestyle or their relationships. We all have different resources for the tools we use in tackling our problems. It can be our upbringing, our traumas, our fears, etc. We rely on our orientation when we decide on the actions we take.

Recognize that the way a person acts is what is right to them and is not meant to disappoint anybody. This is their best. They can improve and make better choices in the future but for now, this is what they can do with the resources that they have.

Sometimes, what you are seeing from someone is the state that they are in and not their character as a person. People go through different things in life and these can sometimes make an impact on their performance.

Here is a situation for you. So you are working on a project with a colleague and he is cranky and he was just not doing well in this task with you. It is easy to get frustrated in a situation like this. But what if you try to figure out what is going on with him first?

You talk to the guy and tell him your concerns kindly. He tells you his daughter is in the hospital and it has been affecting him. Stress can take a toll on a person in a variety of ways. Maybe he was not sleeping well, maybe he has been having physiological issues because of this. There is a lot that can go on when a person is in a difficult situation.

When you find out about this, you try to console him and you tell him to take a breather.

The very next day, your partner comes to work and tells you his daughter has recovered. You see the relief in his face and his whole demeanor has changed. He performed so much better and he made a lot of progress in your project.

Your decision to trust that maybe this person was just in a difficult state turned out right. You could have gotten angry and it might have turned out differently. You could have added more tension in the situation and do irreparable damage to your relationship.

What happened to your workmate can happen to every person. Try to have a little faith in more people and you might see them shine the next day.

2. DIFFERENT PEOPLE, DIFFERENT STANDARDS

Your standards are not the same as everybody else's. When you are too rigid with what you think is right, it can be frustrating to you if another person does not share the same viewpoints as you. People can have different methods and perspectives on things and what works for you might not work for others. If you again look at the actions of others and have faith that they are doing the best they can, then your standards should not apply to them.

By being too fixated on your idea of the right way of doing things, you do not get to see the good in other people's ways. You fail to learn and you fail to show appreciation to those who deserve it.

This is not to say that you should not give advice or suggestions. You can always try to compromise. What you should not do is to invalidate the work of others based on the standards you set.

If your approach is to distrust a person and assume things ahead of their actions, you only lose a bet against yourself. You are putting tension where there is none.

The simplest version of this is when people pronounce things differently. You correct someone and you get annoyed whenever they get it wrong. And then you travel to a place where everybody says it the way that person does. Wouldn't you feel embarrassed by this?

Do not lose the chance to see good in people. You are only disappointing yourself.

3. Maturity Comes at Different Paces

Maturity comes in different forms and at

different paces. Have you ever met a person and taken them to be quite immature?

People can mature in life, career, and relationships. The lessons we get in life depend on the experiences we take. Today, people start making their families at a later age compared to those from the earlier generations. They used to marry in their 20s while today, people prefer to get married in their late 30s or 40s.

Our values take us to our preferred journeys. If you prioritize your career, then you build your career first. If you value relationships, it is easier for you to prioritize loved ones over your career.

If the career woman meets a man who wants to build a family soon, they will surely have conflicting needs. The man can say the woman is not mature enough for him. And the woman can say the same thing about him, too. But the truth is, their maturities are at different places.

If you only see maturity in the form you prefer and the time you set, you will be disappointed in a lot of people. But if you try and see what a person looks for in life and how they place value on things, then maybe you can get to know them for who they truly are.

When you find people you appreciate and who

have become important to your life, do things to acknowledge them. Every person wants to feel accepted and seen by the people they value too.

By showing your appreciation to those who do things you admire, you draw them closer to you and you motivate them to keep doing things they are good at. Not many people will admit it or maybe they are not aware of it, but receiving compliments and thank yous make people feel worthy and fulfilled.

Showing appreciation does not always need to be a grand gesture. Sometimes preparing to make impressive gestures is what takes us away from making the actual move. Remember that this is about the person you appreciate. It is counterproductive to put your ego in showing someone you admire them.

Here are simple ways to show people you appreciate them:

1. Call them by their name. When you call people by their name, it makes people feel acknowledged. Instead of just saying "Hey", including the person's name makes a lot of difference.

2. When you are going out of the office to get coffee. Ask a coworker if he wants

you to get one for him too. It is a simple way of saying you see them working hard and it is okay for you to do something to take some burden off their day.

3. If someone is absent, tell them you missed him at the office and hope he is okay. If there is extra work that needs to be done, don't make an issue out of it. When your coworker gets back after the small gesture you made, he may even work harder.

4. Respect the space you share with others. Do not leave your mess in the spaces that other people use.

5. Always remember to return anything you borrowed and say thank you. Do not inconvenience the lender by waiting for him to check up on you and do not give him the idea that you do not care about his gesture of lending you his item.

6. Everybody makes mistakes. Show people you trust them to make things right. This can be encouraging to people and they will indeed do their best to make up.

7. Celebrate occasions and milestones. Make people see that you care about

them and that you are happy for them
when they make achievements.
Birthdays, promotions, graduations, etc.
These are events when you should
acknowledge people.

8. Say thank you to someone who gives you
an update or a heads up. Say thank you
to any favor or gesture a person does for
you. Let them know you appreciate their
efforts.

9. Give positive feedback. Tough love
should be balanced with good feedback.
How do they know when they are doing
right? And people put in more effort
when they see that others are happy with
their work.

10. Give gifts. A piece of chocolate is a gift, a
cup of coffee is a gift, a compliment is a
gift, a message is a gift. Do something for
others to make them feel you appreciate
them. Not only on special occasions.

11. Make eye contact when someone is
speaking and when you are talking to
somebody. It shows that you are focusing
your attention on them and their
presence and attention are valued.

12. When someone is speaking, get off your phone. Pay attention.

13. Keep your word. If you can't, apologize and give them a heads up. Do not suddenly disappear.

14. Show people you care enough to show up. Show up when invited, show up in meetings, show up on special occasions.

15. Respect other people's time. Try your best not to come in late.

16. Treat others as you want to be treated.

17. When someone is feeling down, a friend, a coworker, or a family member, be there for them. A simple call, a simple message, or even just keeping them company is enough.

18. When they are happy, cherish that moment with them as well. Do not ignore the emotions of those who are important to you. That is when you get to know them more and you learn how to interact with them better.

19. The power of touch. Shake people's hands, give a pat on the back, hug your loved ones. This offers an emotional,

physical, and spiritual connection to
people you appreciate.

20. Tell people you love that you love them.

Those things may seem small but they matter. Know the value of people in your life and acknowledge them. Build and maintain relationships that are meaningful not just for you but for the other person as well. Practice these things and you will slowly feel the difference in the way you view relationships and the way you socially interact with people.

13

FORWARD THINKING AND WILLING TO LET GO OF THE PAST

*N*ow that you have a better view of relationships and you are more aware of your emotional intelligence. There is something you have to learn about relationships as well. Some things just cannot work out.

When this happens, people tend to hold on to the past and regret previous actions. They spend so much time dwelling on the things that did not work out. Learning when and how to let go is a part of social intelligence.

It is not easy to let go of the past. This includes the trauma, bad habits, disillusionment, unhealthy relationships, and toxic people we have encountered before. But did you hear all of that was mentioned? They are all negative experiences.

According to neuroscience, negative and positive information is processed by the brain differently. Since people tend to think about negative experiences in more detail, our brains remember these events better.

We cannot change how our brain processes information but you can train yourself to feed your mind with healthier thoughts.

One way to do this is by cutting off the emotional connection we have with these negative experiences. It is hard to accept when we make mistakes and when we get hurt by other people. We feel weakened by these thoughts and we feel ashamed.

Here are more reasons to move forward and not get stuck in the past:

YOU CAN'T CHANGE THE PAST

There is nothing you can do at this point to take back the words and actions you regret from yours. Punishing yourself with negative emotions will not change your previous actions. What you can change, however, is your present and future circumstances. Take responsibility by making better choices. If you regret an action, then do not make the same mistake again.

MAKE WAY FOR BETTER THINGS

When you fill your life with fear and regret, you have no more space for new experiences that will give you the opportunity to have a better life. Stop holding on to the things that fill your life with hopelessness so that good things will come to you.

YOU IMPROVE YOURSELF

In order to let go of the past, you have to stop making the same decisions. You have to let go of bad habits, toxic people, old frustrations, and other things that keep you from moving on. You have to make an effort to get out of your comfort zone. Yes, your negative experiences are now considered your comfort zone. They become excuses to keep yourself from deciding on a new life. It holds you back from challenging yourself with new goals and building new relationships. Give yourself the chance to find happiness.

EXPERIENCE FREEDOM

Yes, there were snippets of happiness in your previous experiences. However, you were hurt and you have made some mistakes too. It does not erase the happy parts but it just cannot happen without the bad parts. Do not carry the heavy load of your past for the small pieces of happy memories. Free yourself up with the baggage of your past mistakes. Take out the weight one by one so that you can freely move forward.

See how far you have come

You have come so far and your past has given you life lessons that made you a better person today. Embrace who you are now. Nobody is perfect. We have all made mistakes in the past and that made us stronger individuals today. Forgive yourself and see what else the world has to offer. Put all your heart and energy into your aspirations to make your life happier.

Stop losing yourself to your mistakes. Nothing is permanent in this world and that includes the pain and troubles of your bad decisions in the past. Do not let them turn into self-destructing behaviors.

Rumination can take over our lives when we focus on our negative experiences. But If the past cannot be changed, why do you continue to live it? Worry and fear can take over you and influence your actions in the present. Although our past has led us to who we are today, it does not define our future actions and circumstances. Take control of your future and your life.

So, how do you take yourself out of this loop?

1. BE ACCOUNTABLE FOR YOUR PAST

Our negative experiences of the past may have caused us pain and suffering. It is easier to point fingers and find things to blame outside of ourselves. We cannot live with the shame that comes along with our bad decisions. But that is the reason why you keep denying it. You are aware that you have mistakes but you keep finding excuses to justify your wrong actions.

It is hard to trick the mind. If you try to convince yourself of a more ideal version of the past so that you can avoid feeling embarrassed and ashamed, you will not learn how to adjust and better yourself.

Find peace within yourself. Nothing lasts forever and everything can change. If things did not go as you intended them to be, then learn from them. Let go of your failed expectations and build yourself anew.

2. LEARN TO FORGIVE YOURSELF

Being accountable for your mistakes does not mean you shouldn't forgive yourself. In fact, it is an important step to take. When you forgive yourself, you tell yourself that you have done wrong and that you should do better.

Find a way for you to get to a better place. Enjoy your new journey so that your past does not go to waste. Move forward and honor your past by honoring your present. Appreciate what you have now.

3. DO NOT RELY ON THE OPINIONS OF OTHERS

When we think about the other people that played a role in the past, we feel embarrassed and it destroys our self-esteem. Do not get eaten up by this. Their opinion of you has nothing to do with your future actions. If you feel bad that you hurt people, then avoid making the same hurtful actions.

You cannot control what people think of you so just focus on yourself. If it was other people that hurt you in the past, then feel better that you are out of that situation now. Stop letting them continue the pain they have caused you. They are no longer in control of your emotions.

Stop relying on their opinion of you. What is important is that you have made the decision to make your life better. Remind yourself that you must remain authentic to yourself and that you are the only one who can set expectations for yourself.

4. YOU ARE NOT DEFINED BY YOUR STRUGGLES

Your struggles can sometimes act like a vortex. When it becomes overwhelming, it sucks you in and you get trapped. You should not let your problems become your identity. They played a part in forging the person you are today but they do not define your character.

You will not lose yourself if you let go of your past. Everyone does their best with what they have and so do you. As long as you keep your focus on your new life, your decisions will keep getting better and better over time. And that is what defines you and the life you want to live. Mistakes are mistakes. Leave them at that and leave them to the past.

If you keep thinking, I did this and that in the past. Well, yes. And that is why you arc taking the steps you are taking now. Letting go of the past does not mean you are being inauthentic to yourself. You are actually being more true to yourself by admitting that you are no longer happy with that phase in your life. You can now move forward now.

5. REGAIN CONTROL OF YOUR MIND

Our attachments are often the root of the problem. Letting go of your past does not mean it only brought you bad things. That is also not a good way of looking at it. Things did not live to your expectations fully and that was it. You cannot say, "I can't let go of the good memories so I will hold on to everything". Read that again. These things are separate.

When something ends, your suffering is caused by your inability to accept that it has ended. If you think holding on to a toxic relationship is how you can keep the good memories going then prepare yourself to keep the negative experiences going as well. Stop holding on to your expectations.

When you are unable to appreciate the present, you keep going back to the past. Be thankful that you had happy moments in the past. But stop losing your present to the past.

Socially intelligent people take the learnings

from their past failures and apply them to their actions in the present and in the future. We live our lives day by day and we have a chance at new beginnings every day.

It is better to take action so that we can make new decisions that will give us a more meaningful future. We must look forward and let go of our fears and hesitations because there is a lot more to explore. Find your truth and be fair to the people you meet now and the people you will meet in the future. Show them your true self.

14

CONTINUALLY LEARNING AND GROWING TOWARDS INDEPENDENCE

*E*motional and Social Intelligence are lifelong learning endeavors. You must constantly evolve and grow. You have to always be open to new ideas and you must be willing to learn from others. The world continues to change and it is a sign that we as a people are thriving.

While learning from others and having high emotional intelligence is essential to self-development, it can also take your independence away from you. Because you want to keep growing and you want to learn as much as you can, when someone presents an idea that seems like a better fit it makes you think twice about the progress you are making. This in turn can be detrimental to your journey towards self-development.

You must strive to be independent if you want to get the best out of your learning journey. An independent person ultimately trusts himself and his own judgment to make the right decisions for himself. This may seem like an obvious thing to do but most people don't even notice when they have become dependent outside of themselves. Each time you let others influence your decisions for yourself, you have actually started to share the power you have for yourself. While this can be a good thing sometimes, relying on things like this will make it difficult for you to keep your independence.

There are several ways a person could be losing his independence.

You should not allow the opinion of others to be the basis for your self-worth. The decisions you make for your life should come from your authentic self. Your aspirations, your needs, and the relationships you form should be dictated by your own values and beliefs.

Because they are your own, only you can fully understand the decisions you make. Other people will have their own perspective of what's wrong or right but those standards cannot always apply to you. When you let others shape your beliefs and decisions, you slowly lose sight of who you are.

If you always give in to people because you feel guilty, you may have lost your independence to them.

Not being able to attend parties because you want to rest for tomorrow's work is perfectly okay. Not picking up a friend's call because you want some time for yourself is still okay. Saying no to expensive trips because you are paying for bills is definitely okay.

Do not make decisions just because you can't disappoint someone. Go to the party because you want to see people. Pick up the call because you want to have a chat with your friend. Go on that expensive trip because you have earned it. Only make those decisions if you are truly comfortable with them.

If you are friends with everybody, think about the reasons why you are friends with all of those people. Having friends is good for many reasons. One of the goals of honing social intelligence is being able to form strong relationships with others. However, it is also a sign of having great social intelligence if you know that there are people you keep close, there are people you just know, and there are people you stay away from.

Take a look at who your friends are and why they

are in your life. Do not get pressured into entertaining everybody that enters your life. Set boundaries for yourself. You can have many people in your life and still be lonely inside.

Take care of the meaningful relationships you have. Always be kind. But stay away from people who take the life out of you. Do not base your happiness on the number of people around you. Find your own happiness first so you can share it with those who are dear to you.

Holding a grudge is a sign of being reliant on something that has disappointed you. It seems like an odd thing to say but people who hold on to the thought of things that made them upset are not able to let go of the expectations they had that others have failed them with.

Imagine how much time and mental energy you are giving up because of your disappointment with something that did not work out. Instead of wasting your precious energy on rumination, find another channel for your happiness and fulfillment.

Giving up your goals and dreams because you were rejected is being dependent on the approval of others. When people decide to not work with you or when they do not believe in your potential, they base it on their own set of standards. Not yours and not for the whole world. You should not give up your dreams based on that. If you are changing your goals, it must be because you really want to and you have better goals you want to tend to.

Instead of giving up, find another door to knock on or pursue getting better and then go and get another chance at it.

In line with what we just discussed in number 5, proving someone wrong should not be something you think about. When you get rejected or when you get bad remarks from someone else, you do not go and do things for the sake of proving them wrong. Doing this shows that you are dependent on the idea of others about you.

What for? Remember to do things for your life's fulfillment and your authentic self.

When you talk about others a lot, you show how much power they have over your life. Why spend time and energy discussing people who annoy you and play no role in your life's goals? Do not let thinking and talking about people who don't matter take your focus out of the things you want to do in life.

Blaming other people for your bad decisions will only make you lose control of your choices in life. When you make decisions for yourself, you make them because you have your own values system that you follow.

Pointing fingers just sound like an excuse if you claim others took the best out of you. If you are dealing with a toxic person, recognize that they don't fit in your life. Do not dread the "mistake" you made with them. Take control of your situation and make the right choices for yourself.

Giving too much credence to people will only set you on a confusing path. Keep yourself at the helm and go off in the direction that your true self has chosen for you.

If you seem to have grown dependent on others, there's no need to worry. It happens to the best of us. You have to know that it is never too late to regain control of your life. You need to make the conscious effort to be able to think, feel, and act in a way that is helpful to your life's journey.

Some people are scared of the idea that if they do not go out seeking the approval of others that they are becoming too selfish. Says who? But anyway, you can think about it this way, you are doing this because you want to offer people your true best. You want to be the happiest and the most fulfilled you can be that is authentic to you and that will be authentic to them.

Set yourself out on the path of independence so that you can be genuine to everyone you welcome into your life.

Here are some additional thoughts on claiming autonomy in your life.

1. KNOW YOURSELF BETTER

You always start with this. This time, your reason for getting to know yourself is because you might not know what you are capable of, yet. Many people who rely on the ideas of others do so because they lack trust in themselves. Do things that will increase your self-esteem and self-worth so that you can have faith that your decisions are right for you.

If you end up making mistakes, you do not make others responsible for them and you adjust yourself because you want to do better. The only way to find your strengths and weaknesses is by taking risks. It is okay to find guidance from others but make sure they resonate with your truth.

When you operate your life this way, you regret nothing and you find fulfillment sooner.

2. CHALLENGE YOUR DOUBTS AND BELIEFS

Our lives are continually evolving. Sometimes the things that were valid to us before are no longer true at a certain point in our lives. Always stop and check if you still want the same things before you make a decision. We all grow and we all change. See to it that you are not choosing things out of habit.

If your priorities and your beliefs can change, confront your doubts as well. Seek the truths in the life you live in and never let your doubts rule your life.

3. TAKE RESPONSIBILITY

If you take responsibility for your needs, no one needs to take over for you and you truly spend time with people for who they are more than what you need from them. When people are in a codependent relationship, they become good at meeting each others' needs. The problem comes when they forget to be good at getting their individual needs.

While it is great to have someone who can be truly selfless and who is there for you when you need them, it is wrong to fully rely on them. Take note of your own needs and find ways to meet them.

4. ASSERT YOURSELF

Set healthy boundaries and communicate your needs well. Assertiveness is not equal to arrogance. You can be assertive and respectful at the same time. Just the same as you respect others, you must respect yourself too.

Your ideas and your beliefs matter and can be helpful to others too. If you can assert yourself while being respectful to others, you can offer your full self to those who matter.

We are responsible for our own growth and happiness. Other people can be instrumental to our self-discovery but we are still in control of the path we take.

15

BE RELENTLESSLY POSITIVE

There are positive people and then there are negative people. People are drawn to those with a positive worldview in general. People see you in a negative light when you have a negative outlook. Who wants to work with someone who is demotivating and critical all the time?

If your talent is to make everything look worse than what it is, it will be difficult for you to understand yourself and others. Why? Because you actively search for the negative things. Effective leaders share positivity.

Research shows that pessimistic people are actually more at risk of having heart disease. And people who have a more positive outlook perform better at work. Positivity shows a lot of benefits but many people have a hard time adopting a positive mindset.

It was mentioned earlier that when you think about negative things your brain goes into hyper-focus and it will retain the negativity once they are processed. Have you ever noticed that when you start thinking about something bad it gets worse and worse in your head?

One reason why it becomes harder for some people to be positive is that they misconstrue posi-tivity for happiness or being jolly. They think happi-ness is a prerequisite to positivity. That is why some people say, "You cannot expect positivity from me because I am very sad/angry about my situation". Yes, it is more difficult to be optimistic when you are sad or angry. But this is because you ruminate when you accommodate negative thoughts.

Positivity and emotions are not in the same cate-gory of things. When you are positive, you search for solutions, you look forward to good results, and you aim for happiness. The goal of being positive can be a variety of things. Happiness can both be a goal and effect of being positive but it is not a prerequisite.

It also becomes difficult if you think about posi-tivity as some sort of a bet or wishful thinking. It makes it look like an imaginary and impractical outlook on life. However, positive thinking is actually a method. You are not merely taking a chance or putting things at risk. Positivity is a method and there are steps to it.

Positivity is also not something you are either born with or without. Staying positive is intentional and it requires constant effort. You have to change your perspective and begin to think positively. There are methods to it that you can practice.

Here are some techniques you can try:

1. EXERCISE REGULARLY, EAT, AND SLEEP WELL.

People often take these things for granted but it is probably the most practical way to become positive. Fact is, when your body is in top shape, it is easier for you to think positively.

When you are hungry, your body releases hormones that make you angry and stressed. This is why "hangry" is a thing. Exercising is also a type of meditation and it can keep your mind away from rumination. Lack of sleep also messes up with your mindset and stress levels.

When your body is also in top shape, you feel

more in control of your life and your self-esteem is higher. This helps keep your stress levels lower.

2. START YOUR DAY RIGHT

When you start your day right, it creates a domino effect and everything follows.

Sleep is also a main factor here. If you have enough sleep, you wake up feeling recharged and ready to take on your day.

Try to set a good sleeping schedule as well so that you avoid rushing yourself to work. Getting stressed because of the rush might set the tone of your day to a bad one. Getting late also makes you feel like you are not in control and you go back to having negative thoughts.

3. DON'T RUSH

Whenever you rush things, you become a bit more reckless and it can create a lot of stress.

Always try to plan things with a good schedule so that your mind can concentrate on actual work versus the pressure of being rushed.

If you are already in the moment of rushing

things, try to take bits of breathers so that you can refocus between tasks.

4. CULTIVATE A POSITIVE ENVIRONMENT

Choose the people you spend time with. It is hard to become positive when you are with toxic people. It is the same thing with the things you read, watch, and listen to.

Follow sites that produce healthy content that you can learn from. Watch films that offer you a better outlook in life. Listen to music that can help your mind focus.

5. BE GRATEFUL

Think about the things you are grateful for and say thank you to those who bring positive experiences to your life. Say thank you even for the little things. It does not sound like much but actually saying those two words can be powerful enough to remind you of the good things in your life.

6. IT CAN BE DONE

When your mind goes into this whirlwind of hopelessness, stop. Say it in your mind and stop everything that you are doing.

After that, breathe and refocus. You will not get the solution right away but instead of telling yourself that it is impossible, ask yourself how it can be done. Then, work your way towards finding a solution.

7. ARE YOUR FEARS REAL?

Our brain is really smart and it can even trick us. When we ruminate, it has a great way of convincing us that our fears are real when they actually aren't. Most of the negative thoughts you have are products of how your brain processed an initial fear.

It is a trap. Think about the fears you had before. How many of them became true?

Ask yourself what is the worst that can happen from this and then what can you do about it?

To get ahead in life you have no choice but to get out of your comfort zone. Believe in yourself. You have come this far.

8. HELP SOMEONE OUT

If you can't seem to be positive for yourself, try to bring positivity to someone else. When you do things for other people, it brings a sense of pride and hope for yourself. When you make someone happy and you help them out in a situation, it brings lightness to your life and it creates a positive trend in your mind.

9. DON'T TAKE THINGS PERSONALLY

Sometimes getting feedback can be taken negatively. Don't. Criticism cannot be avoided because we are humans and we all have different ways of tackling things. If it is unavoidable, there is no point in fearing it.

Keep yourself calm and listen to the feedback. Take what is useful and do not take it personally. Plus, not all feedback is about you. Remind yourself that people have differing standards.

10. IMPROVE YOUR SELF-ESTEEM AND SELF-AWARENESS

We always go back to this because social intelligence is about understanding yourself and others. If you know yourself well, you cannot be fazed by anything that is out of what you stand for.

Always go back to your goals in life and your own journey as a person and see what actions you can take to achieve them. Sometimes daydreaming helps to remind you of your goals. Take some time off and then think about the things that you want for yourself.

Will those things be affected by your current problems? Ten years down the road, will these things still matter?

11. BE MINDFUL

Make an effort to see little things that make your day better. It may seem hard when you are in a bad situation but think simply.

Take a little walk and explore. I came up with a method I have for myself. I call this funneling. When my mind is filled with things to do, difficult tasks, fears, etc., I go into haywire. So what I do is I find an easy activity like walking or playing simple puzzles.

My mind is distracted enough but it does not stop me from thinking about my tasks. What happens is there is much less space for my brain to entertain more negativity. My small activities act as a funnel so that I can streamline my thoughts.

Sometimes distractions can be too overwhelming and you end up escaping from your tasks. That is not the goal of this exercise. When you procrastinate it only piles up the anxieties you had to begin with.

Find small things that take a little bit of space in your mind and then try it out.

This works for me and it may or may not work for you. The point is, you have to release yourself from negativity because it never creates anything good in your life.

When you make the conscious effort to change your perspective on things, a lot of other things will follow. You find better ways of handling toxic work relations. You find it easier to deal with hectic schedules.

Positivity should also not be looked at as an expectation. When you are drifting away from that positive feeling, do not get pressured into bringing yourself to the "ideal" level again. Breathe. Start somewhere, start small, and then inch your way out of negativity.

16

LOOK FOR WAYS TO MAKE LIFE MORE FUN, HAPPY, AND INTERESTING

When you look for opportunities to find happiness and fulfillment with others, you tend to achieve it for yourself more easily. Whether it is in the workplace, at home, or with friends, you can receive pleasure and satisfaction from seeing others happy and fulfilled.

Spreading a culture of having fun and making things interesting helps everybody including yourself. When there is no fun in the things you do, they become pointless and monotonous. Soon enough you will start to resent things.

People do things because they want a better life. You work because you want financial stability. you work harder because you aim for fulfillment. You get into a romantic relationship because you want to have joy with the person you love.

No one will ever be motivated if you offer them a difficult and miserable life. If you are a person who knows yourself well and is confident enough to face life head-on, you enjoy seeing others achieve their goals. There is no point in wanting people to suffer.

When you make people happy, they want to do more and they become more loyal to you. They want to thrive with you because you let them enjoy life more. And that is what fulfillment is all about. Everyone thrives and everyone achieves something while doing things that make them feel more like themselves.

And because you allow them to achieve their goals with you, they trust you and they trust themselves more. When a person is surrounded by trust and positivity, they become more confident and they take more risks. Taking risks leads to more opportunities and progress for everybody.

When you are in a relationship with a significant other or your family members, celebrate their achievements with them. Allow and encourage them to confidently take on a project or go for that dream job. You do not go into a relationship to see someone trapped in insecurity and hesitation. Let them love themselves more and love them for who they are.

In the office, you should still celebrate achievements. If someone does well, it will be good for the company so everybody wins. Aspire for greatness without pulling anyone down. Be grateful for the opportunity you have in the company you are in and let the company thrive so you can fly high as well.

Seeing others achieve things for themselves will not take opportunities away from you. You are responsible for your own success. Do not ever think you deserve something more than others. You do not know what other people put up with and the hard work that they do. Just the same, you are the only one who knows what effort you put into your work. So understand that you all go through different paths in life and offer a little more kindness. People tend to pay kindness forward so more and more people will thrive.

Fun does not always mean you have to do silly things and laugh all the time. Fun comes from different things for different people. The only thing that is common with fun is the enjoyment that comes with it. And when you make an effort for someone to enjoy things with you, they feel valued and acknowledged.

To create fun, you have to get to know people. You have to spend time with them and pay attention to what moves them. When you understand someone, it becomes easier for you to create moments of fun with them.

Some people find fun in food and conversations. Others like to do physical activities like sports. There are people who find relaxing activities fun. It all depends on the person you want to spend time with. And don't worry, sometimes just showing someone that you want to enjoy things with them is enough to make someone feel valued. Do not feel too bad if you think you didn't do well.

If you are having trouble thinking of ways to bring fun to your life and other people's lives, there are some ways you can remind yourself of fun times.

CREATE A DAYDREAM JOURNAL

Write down the things you enjoy. From something as simple as popping your fingers to something as big as buying a new care. When you write things down, imagine being able to experience those things you wrote down. As you imagine yourself in those situations, find out which ones give you the most natural fun reactions. Some of them will make you smile, some of them will make you feel silly. Take the emotions you had from this exercise and realize the things that are fun to you.

GO BACK TO YOUR CHILDHOOD

Children tend to be more carefree with the way they have fun and enjoy things. That is why research suggests that our preferences on the things we find fun in are formed when we were just kids. Daydreaming every once in a while about your childhood fun will remind you of the things you like and how pure, innocent fun feels like.

One more thing that people should pursue is to live a life that is interesting to them. Every person should work hard for their dreams and goals but no one should forget about keeping things interesting. When you do things that take the monotony out of your work, the task becomes more exciting and you want to keep going.

It is the same thing with relationships. If you treat relationships like a transaction where people just act according to their functions, it becomes forgettable and it can create a lot of resentments between people. Sooner or later, people will just want to move on because they no longer feel a sense of joy in what they are doing. Remember the goals you set in your relationships. If you want to be with someone because you want to be happy with them, then do not take time for granted.

When I was a kid, my dad wanted me and my brother to catalog all our books and arrange them on the shelves. We had tons of books and my brother and I wanted to skip the whole thing. We were dreading having to work on it because it was just boring and it will take a lot of time.

When the time came for us to work on it, my dad brought out a cooler of drinks and a bag of snacks with him. We suddenly felt excited about the task and we wanted to do more. After we were done arranging the books, my brother and I wanted another task to work on.

My dad always tried to make boring tasks interesting to us. I have enjoyed chores growing up because of him. It did not feel like a bribe if that is what it seemed to you. My dad knew what we liked and he wanted us to enjoy. We would have done it anyway even without the surprise because we had no choice. We were his kids after all. But my dad knew he had to make it interesting for us so that we can learn a better way of working.

I brought that lesson with me ever since. There is nothing to lose when you make work more interesting. It just makes things lighter and more enjoyable. And because I had that positive experience, I try to bring that culture everywhere I go.

There is a lot of happiness and fulfillment in seeing others enjoy and do well. Only people who have a good understanding of who they are and who are able to manage the way they think and feel can truly be satisfied when others are at a good place in their life.

If one person has not been able to fulfill his life goals yet, it should not matter if other people are able to achieve theirs sooner. In fact, there is hope in seeing others succeed. You can learn from them and you can be braver at taking risks yourself.

You define the life you want to live and you design the mind you want to have. Surround yourself with happiness and positivity and you can slowly see yourself experiencing those very things for yourself too.

Social intelligence is not just about yourself and the things you want to achieve. It involves the people around you. When you try to understand the people around you more, you get better at managing relationships with them. As a result, you will be surrounded by happy people who are able to spread happiness as well. This changes the culture in your organization, in your community, in your family, and within your friendships.

CONCLUSION

Throughout the book, it has been a recurring task to get to know yourself better. This is because everything starts with you. To understand people, you have to have a better sense of yourself first. Identify the good, the bad, and the ugly in you.

When you know where your identity starts and where it ends, you no longer get confused when people start to have opinions about you. Take note of your social liabilities and continue to practice being real.

Once you open yourself up to other people, prepare to have your values and beliefs challenged. We are all human and we were raised in many different ways. Our culture and the values system of the societies we come from can have a deeply rooted influence on us.

That is why when we confront our differences with other people, we must strive to be respectful and understanding of the things we say and do. The only way to resolve conflict is if we open ourselves to the idea that we all have needs and it is our own responsibility to communicate them well so that we can all be understood.

You are now equipped with the steps to take to be able to practice effective communication. You must put them to good use because one of the biggest challenges of the world today is filling up the gaps between the differences in our cultures.

As much as we would like to be heard and paid attention to, our peers also have the same amount of needs as we do. Pay attention to them and listen with intent.

In that case, we must practice patience and kindness and set our energies to resolution and maintaining relationships rather than in winning. What is the point of winning if you lose valuable people to things that will not even matter in the grand scheme of things? What we must win at is being able to resolve our conflicts with others. That we are able to meet the needs of one another through effective and respectful discussions.

The key towards having meaningful relationships is when we make a conscious effort to recognize a person's value and acknowledge them for this. There is no way for you to foster worthwhile connections if you fail to appreciate people.

If you are able to accept other people for who they are and not for their troubles, then give the same kindness to yourself too. Do not punish yourself by continuing to live in the past because of the embarrassment and regrets your previous mistakes have given you.

Allow yourself to grow and feel your social intelligence kicking in. There is nowhere else to go but forward.

You are not defined by your past. Nor are you defined by the opinions of others about you. Regain control of your life by realizing that what matters is the actions you will take for your present and for your future. You have to take yourself out of the vicious cycle because it is more worthwhile to focus on your development as a person. Create space for the new learning you will receive.

If there are people to keep, there are also people to keep away from.

Remember to keep yourself aware of people who will consume you out of your energy. It is part of your emotional and social intelligence to protect you from people who are disrespecting you. Exit yourself gracefully from such relationships and focus on other things that resonate more with your genuine self.

When you find people who you value in your life, share with them your happiness and enjoy things with them. What is the point of relationships if you do not live a happy life with each other? Make it your goal to be positive and then happy.

Every person wants to do well in life and find a way for them to have the happiness they long for. Continue to practice kindness especially to those who are still in their dark place. If you once been in a dark place, then you will understand what kindness can do to a person who is struggling.

You can only say you are content and fulfilled with your own life if you are able to celebrate the achievements of other people sincerely.

Be positive that you can do many things on your own and that you are the master of your life. Social intelligence is not about getting ahead of people. It is about understanding people and how you can be able to live a more meaningful and rewarding life through the relationships you foster with them. Use your learnings to spread more positivity and support others so that we can all thrive.

.

John Ward is a professor, a motivational speaker, an author, and holds two degrees in psychology and neuroscience. He has devoted his life to helping people become their best selves both in the classroom and in countless books.

With his background in behavioral sciences and developmental psychology, John has managed to help numerous people overcome their self-defeating habits in order to become better individuals. He has been a star speaker at self-improvement conferences, local centers for the underprivileged, and sometimes even at college graduations. John wishes to help as many people transform their lives for the better before he himself turns fifty years old.

When he's not writing or teaching, John enjoys traveling the world with his adoring wife of almost twenty years by his side. And because John is a family man, first and foremost, he enjoys spending the free time that he has, with his family. He is proud to father two amazing and successful sons, one of whom, wishes to follow in his father's footsteps and become a motivational speaker himself.

REFERENCES

Ainomugisha, G. (2020, May 15). 5 Great Reasons Why Happiness Increases Productivity. The 6Q Blog. https://inside.6q.io/5-great-reasons-why-happiness-increases-productivity/

BBC - Ethics - Lying. (n.d.). Bbc.Co.Uk. http://www.bbc.co.uk/ethics/lying/lying_1.shtml

Borchard, T. (2009, October 27). 5 Emotional Vampires & How to Combat Them. Psychcentral.Com. https://psychcentral.com/blog/5-emotional-vampires-and-how-to-combat-them/

Bradberry, T. (2016, September 3). 3 Powerful Ways To Stay Positive. Forbes. https://www.forbes.com/sites/travisbradberry/2016/08/23/3-powerful-ways-to-stay-positive/#4f873a6819c9

Cherry, K., & Tust, A. (2020, May 3). Introspection and How It Is Used In Psychology Research. Verywell Mind. https://www.verywellmind.com/what-is-introspection-2795252

Communication Skills. (n.d.). Https://Www.Skillsyouneed.Com/. https://www.skillsyouneed.com/ips/communication-skills.html

Conceiving The Idea Of A Pony Express. (n.d.). Britannica.Com. https://www.britannica.com/topic/Pony-Express/Conceiving-the-idea-of-a-Pony-Express

Daum, K. (2014, July 10). 9 Simple Ways You Can Show Appreciation. Inc.Com. https://www.inc.com/ss/kevin-daum/9-ways-to-show-appreciation

Deutschendorf, H. (2017, April 12). 7 Habits of Highly Emotionally Intelligent People. Fast Company. https://www.fastcompany.com/3028712/7-habits-of-highly-emotionally-intelligent-people

Digestive Health Team. (2020, March 14). Is Being 'Hangry' Really a Thing — or Just an Excuse? Health Essentials from Cleveland Clinic. https://health.clevelandclinic.org/is-being-hangry-really-a-thing-or-just-an-excuse/

Edberg, H. (2020, July 27). How to Stay Posi-

tive: 11 Smart Habits. The Positivity Blog. https://
www.positivityblog.com/how-to-stay-positive/

Greer, A. (2016, April 1). Stop Letting Other
People's Opinions Control You. Www.Huffpost.-
Com. https://www.huffpost.com/entry/stop-letting-
other-peoples-opinions-control-you_b_9587330

Horton, A. P. (2019, September 16). The 7-day
guide to improving your social intelligence. Fast
Company.   https://www.fastcompany.com/
90403912/the-7-day-guide-to-improving-your-
social-intelligence

How Positive Thinking Builds Skills, Boosts
Health, and Improves Work. (2020, February 4).
James   Clear.   https://jamesclear.com/positive-
thinking

How to improve social intelligence. (2018,
August 24). Factual. https://blogs.harvard.edu/
factual/improve-social-intelligence/

Koifman, N. (2014, June 30). Why You Should
Try and Be "Authentic." Hufftingtonpost.Ca.
https://www.huffingtonpost.ca/natasha-koifman/
authentic_b_5543874.html

Lehmacher, W. (2019, October 17). What does
it mean to respect cultural diversity? - Quora [Forum
Post]. Quora.Com. https://www.quora.com/What-
does-it-mean-to-respect-cultural-diversity

Mirfattah, S. (2017, May 18). 10 Easy Ways to Increase Your Social Intelligence and Motivate Your People. Linkedin. https://www.scribbr.com/apa-citation-generator/new/book/

Morin, A., & Snyder, C. (2020, April 8). Strategies to Help You Develop Social Intelligence Skills. Verywell Mind. https://www.verywellmind.com/what-is-social-intelligence-4163839

Razzetti, G. (2019, September 16). How to Be Authentic in A Fake World. Liberationist - Change Leadership. https://liberationist.org/how-to-be-authentic-in-a-fake-world/

Razzetti, G. (2020, February 13). How to Let Go of the Past. Www.Psychologytoday.Com. https://www.psychologytoday.com/us/blog/the-adaptive-mind/202002/how-let-go-the-past

Roelink, M. (2015, May 13). 5 Reasons Why You Should Let Go of the Past. Www.Recoverywarriors.Com. https://www.recoverywarriors.com/5-reasons-why-you-should-let-go-of-the-past/

Santiago, R. (2015, March 10). How To Save Yourself From Emotional Vampires (Because They're Ruining Your Life). Bustle. https://www.bustle.com/articles/48246-how-to-save-yourself-from-emotional-vampires-because-theyre-ruining-your-life

Segal, J., Robinson, L., & Smith, M. (2019, June). Conflict Resolution Skills - HelpGuide.org. Helpguide.Org. https://www.helpguide.org/articles/relationships-communication/conflict-resolution-skills.htm

Smith, E. (2017, January 11). The Secret to a Meaningful Life is Meaningful Relationships. Www.Gottman.Com. https://www.gottman.com/blog/secret-meaningful-life-meaningful-relationships/

Stinson, A. (2018, March 17). How To Not Let Someone Else's Mood Affect You, According To Experts. Elite Daily. https://www.elitedaily.com/p/how-to-not-let-someone-elses-mood-affect-you-according-to-experts-8500963

Tartakovsky, M. (2018, July 8). 6 Ways to Become More Independent, Less Codependent. Psychcentral.Com. https://psychcentral.com/blog/6-ways-to-become-more-independent-less-codependent/

Whalen, D. (2018, February 27). 6 Ways To Better Appreciate Others - Daniel Whalen. Medium. https://medium.com/@DanielJWhalen/6-ways-to-better-appreciate-others-3e95a5962482

Zalani, P. (2016, June 30). 7 Scientifically-Backed Ways to Improve Social Intelligence.

Turnedtwenty.Com.   https://turnedtwenty.com/7-scientifically-backed-ways-improve-social-intelligence/